Character Education

Education

43 Fitness Activities for Community Building

Don R. Glover, MA
University of Wisconsin, River Falls

Leigh Ann Anderson, MA
Saint Mary's University

Human Kinetics

Library of Congress Cataloging-in-Publication Data

Glover, Donald R.
  Character education : 43 fitness activities for community building /
Don R. Glover, Leigh Ann Anderson.
      p. cm.
Includes bibliographical references (p.).
  ISBN 0-7360-4504-X (Soft Cover)
  1. Moral education (Elementary) 2. Physical education for
children--Study and teaching (Elementary)--Activity programs. 3.
Teamwork (Sports) I. Anderson, Leigh Ann, 1969- II. Title.
  LC268 .G56 2003
  370.11'3--dc21
                                   2002151790

ISBN: 0-7360-4504-X

Acquisitions Editor: Bonnie Pettifor; **Developmental Editor:** Jennifer L. Walker;
Assistant Editors: Sandra Merz Bott, Amanda S. Ewing and Derek Campbell;
Copyeditor: Scott Jerard; **Proofreader:** Sue Fetters; **Permission Manager:** Dalene
Reeder; **Graphic Designer:** Nancy Rasmus; **Graphic Artist:** Denise Lowry; **Photo
Manager:** Leslie A. Woodrum; **Cover Designer:** Nancy Rasmus; **Photographer
(cover):** © Gopher Sport/Kim Poliszuk; **Photographer (interior):** Leslie A. Woodrum,
unless otherwise noted; **Art Manager:** Kelly Hendren; **Illustrator:** Angela K. Snyder;
Printer: Versa Press

Printed in the United States of America   10   9   8   7   6   5   4   3   2   1

Human Kinetics
Web site: www.HumanKinetics.com

United States: Human Kinetics, P.O. Box 5076, Champaign, IL 61825-5076
800-747-4457
e-mail: humank@hkusa.com

Canada: Human Kinetics, 475 Devonshire Road Unit 100, Windsor, ON N8Y 2L5
800-465-7301 (in Canada only)
e-mail: orders@hkcanada.com

Europe: Human Kinetics, 107 Bradford Road, Stanningley, Leeds LS28 6AT,
United Kingdom
+44 (0) 113 255 5665
e-mail: hk@hkeurope.com

Australia: Human Kinetics, 57A Price Avenue, Lower Mitcham, South Australia 5062
08 8277 1555
e-mail: liahka@senet.com.au

New Zealand: Human Kinetics, P.O. Box 105-231, Auckland Central
09-523-3462
e-mail: hkp@ihug.co.nz

To my grandson Josh

I can hardly wait to see all the new things you will be able to do in the next fifteen years.

To Mark

You are an amazing husband and father. The boys and I are so lucky to have you in our lives. I love you.

Contents

Preface

We wrote this book because we feel strongly that physical educators need to spread the word that it is equally important to make our physical education classrooms a place where kids can make not only a fitness connection but also an emotional connection as well. If our students are to engage in and enjoy an active lifestyle as adults, then they have to remember how activity (that is, physical education class) made them feel as youngsters, and we want those memories to be positive, self-affirming, and motivating.

Our Vision

In our vision of the future, we see every child looking forward to physical education class. We see children understanding what activity can do for them, and we see each child intrinsically motivated to participate in whatever physical activity interests them. We feel our vision has a much better chance to become reality if physical educators know how to develop a sense of **community** among their students. We think our vision will be much harder to accomplish if students do not feel like a valued member of the physical education class.

The term *community* implies many things. It implies that there is an environment where people care for and emotionally support one another, regardless of skill level. The term *community* is being used more and more in the academic classroom, and we think it needs to be included in the physical education setting. We see each child more willing to learn if the content is meaningful, if they are involved in their learning, and if they have a voice in the classroom. Intrinsic motivation, according to Kilpatrick, Hebert, and Jacobson (2002), is the most desirable level of motivation. Intrinsic motivation exists when a person chooses to engage in an activity for the sake of the activity, rather than for any external reason. Specifically, in our vision for the future of physical education, intrinsic motivation will be enhanced through the following methods and ideas:

- We see each child acknowledged and recognized when entering the physical education environment, making physical education a more welcoming place to be.

- We see each child become a valued member of a team and always supported and encouraged by that team.
- We see that all students know that the teacher and their teammates care about them.
- We see teachers constantly looking for better ways to connect with kids physically, mentally, and emotionally.
- We see teachers finding new ways to assess students in physical education, using assessment techniques that are based not on genetic skill or strength, but rather portfolio assessments that enable students to look deeper into setting personal goals and developing their own practice plans.
- We see kids making choices about units of study and skills that they want to pursue—another sure way to empower kids and turn them on to activity!
- We see that students' integrity and character will be strengthened by attending physical education class.
- We see our future students becoming more active and looking forward to always being active.

By following the template in this book, we feel that you can reach many more students in a positive way and thus reduce the rising trend toward unhealthy activities, stagnation, and obesity. Specifically, our plan includes the following objectives:

- Increase the number of physical education programs.
- Provide student choice within the physical education curriculum.
- Welcome every student to class with an enthusiastic motivator.
- Put the students into teams at the beginning of the year, and keep these teams together all year.
- Teach the teams how to praise and encourage one another.
- Provide character-education activities for large groups, as well as individual teams.
- Change large-group warm-ups into smaller team warm-ups.
- Do team-building challenges as the first unit of the year.
- Change assessment practices to include portfolio assessment.
- Provide a safe, nonthreatening atmosphere for all students, regardless of their athletic ability.

White House Is Finally on the Right Exercise Track

Last week President Bush announced his "Healthier US Initiative, " a fitness agenda meant to get Americans to stop counting french fries as a major food group and start moving a little bit each day. Though the President himself can run an impressive 6:45 mile, his plan to mobilize the American metabolism is starting with baby steps.

"How about just walking 30 minutes a day?" he offered at last week's kick-off. "That's pretty simple."

You can't argue that this country needs a good kick in the pants, when Krispy Kreme openings merit widespread media coverage and when operating a joystick is the only resistance training most kids get on a regular basis. Still, this White House initiative seems somewhat ironic, since it's my personal theory that much of our current sloth and inactivity can be traced directly back to the Oval Office—specifically to the Presidential Physical Fitness Award.

Some of you may be too young to recall this particular humiliation meted out to our nation's young, so let me offer a short history lesson. Back in 1956, President Dwight D. Eisenhower was alarmed to learn that European kids beat American kids on a battery of physical fitness tests, and so he created the President's Council on Youth Fitness, in a Sputnik-like spirit of catch-up. (He then spent the rest of his presidency modeling good fitness behavior on the golf course.)

A few years later, John F. Kennedy, whose back was so out of whack that he is said to have soldiered through those south lawn football games only with the help of serious tranquilizers, decided to expand the mission to all ages, renaming it the Council on Physical Fitness. By 1966, Lyndon Johnson, a president whom it is impossible to imagine in track shorts, created an award program, administered by the nation's gym teachers, in which grade-schoolers were lined up each spring and forced through a battery of long jumps and push-ups.

In my school, the physical fitness test took on the terrifying import of a hazing ritual. There were stories of boys who ran so hard they barfed. Tales of girls who lunged so far on the long jump that they knocked out their own teeth. Rumors of wimps who couldn't hold their own body weight on the bent-arm hang, and who were so ridiculed they actually had to switch schools.

When our gym teacher came to class with a clipboard and a stopwatch one day, we all knew what was up. Two boys with Audrey Hepburn arms suddenly developed stomachaches that required immediate attention in the nurse's office. One prepubescent girl borrowed an excuse from her older sister's repertoire and claimed she was getting a visit from

(continued)

A new vision of physical activity *and* physical education is taking shape both at the national and local levels.

Reprinted, by permission, from L. Billings, 2002, *White House Finally on the Right Exercise Track*, 25 June, St. Paul Pioneer Press.

(continued)

her Aunt Martha. The rest of us put our heads down as we were put through the paces—running, jumping, lifting, squatting.

This is when the words "exercise" and "punishment" first became synonymous in my mind.

The apex of this ordeal was the bent-arm hang—a skill that, like algebra, has served no useful purpose in real life. We were made to sit on the waxed gym floor and wait for our names to be called alphabetically, at which point we were hoisted up to the bar and timed as all of our classmates watched.

I still remember the boy who couldn't manage to hang on a single second; he went on to have a drug problem in junior high. I remember the poignant struggling of the shortest kid in our class, who wriggled himself up so violently that his elbows went over the bar. He hung there by his armpits, red-faced, until the gym teacher finally unhooked him. The chubby girl in our class surprised us all by hanging on, but her body wiggled in embarrassing places as she struggled to stay aloft.

Oh, the humanity . . . the humanity!

Thank goodness President Bush is showing a kinder, gentler approach to fitness education, exhorting us to walk a little bit, maybe throw the ball around in the back yard before dinner. Kids who want a Presidential Sports Award can now do it on their own time by submitting a personal fitness log and getting an adult to sign off on it. This might take some of the muscle out of the exercise education, but it might also foster a healthier relationship with phys ed than many in my generation had.

I could write about this all day, but I've got to keep my appointment in the weight room. I've got some unresolved issues with my gym teacher that I'm still trying to work out.

Connecting Helps Meet NASPE Standards 5, 6, and 7

Each of these objectives listed here also corresponds to initiatives outlined in NASPE Standards 5, 6, and 7. For example, Standard 5 encourages the development of social and personal responsibility. Kids who feel connected naturally take more responsibility for their own and others' well-being and development. The time they spend in your class is spent more cooperatively and productively. The approach that is explained and modeled in this book also helps students understand and respect differences among themselves (Standard 6). Connected students appreciate and value what each individual contributes to a team. You will see this in both how they learn to act and speak. In addition, *Character Education: 43 Fitness Activities for Community Building* will help students see physical activity as enjoyable, challenging, and socially stimulating (Standard 7). Naturally, your classes will be more fun if students feel welcome, valued, and connected through physical activity. This positive association will help students adopt and maintain a physically active lifestyle throughout their lives. Not only will you see students move toward achieving these standards, you will also empower them to *continue to grow* in each of these targeted areas both in class and in life!

Organization

Now, let's look at the chapters and how they will help you on the path to understanding and creating a character education-centered physical education class focused on enthusiasm, teamwork, and physical fitness.

Chapter 1 Brain Research and Competition in Physical Education

One of the first and best ways to understand the needs and benefits of students is to start on the inside—specifically, their minds and how they work. This chapter outlines the basic biology of the brain and the body's reaction to both positive and negative experiences. It carefully outlines approaches to making physical education classes more "brain friendly" and gives specific guidance for creating positive and meaningful results from potentially stressful situations like competitive games or team selections in your class.

Chapter 2 Motivators, Huddles, and Warm-Ups

We feel that team building is one important step a school can take in providing character instruction for students. But providing character education in the form of motivation, enthusiasm, and empathy for others is a primary responsibility of all school staff. Character education by example provides a friendly environment that fosters respect and a genuine caring attitude by the staff. Chapter 2 provides you with more specific activities physical educators can use to enhance character education, intrinsic motivation, and real enthusiasm for physical activity. Providing team-building activities and character-education activities can go a long way toward fostering students' feelings of acceptance and belonging.

Chapter 3 Team Building

Team Building Through Physical Challenges and *More Team Building Challenges* were published by Human Kinetics in the early 1990s. These books were written to help students learn how to become cooperative and respectful teammates by learning to work together to solve problems. It has been 10 years since the first team-building book came out, and what we have seen since that time is an enthusiastic acceptance of our ideas and the important role team building plays in the physical education curriculum. We have learned that team building is not just a passing trend; it is here to stay! In Chapter 3, we will look at some new team-building activities designed to both challenge and unite students in the pursuit of increased physical activity and sportsmanship. For now, let's remember that the responsibility for teaching young people to be respectful, decent competitors and teammates falls directly on our profession. Team building is an ideal vehicle for meeting this challenge.

Chapter 4 Portfolio Assessment

In regular education classes, students are allowed to bring home books and other materials to further their growth. Are students allowed to do the same in physical education? Unless we are prepared to allow students to check out nets and volleyballs so that they can practice at home, can we honestly grade them on volleyball skills? Chances are that students do not get enough practice in physical education class. We can assess children's fitness and skill levels, but should we really give them a grade based on that assessment? What happens is that many teachers end up simply giving a grade based upon genetics. So the question becomes, Can physical educators find an assessment tool that will motivate students to improve? Chapter 4 explores assessment techniques that will empower children and motivate them to improve.

Your Assignment

Teamwork. Motivation. Enthusiasm. Character. Empowerment. Success. This is our vision of the future for physical education—an environment that does not solely concentrate on fitness and competition, but rather fitness, skill acquisition, social skills, team building, student growth, character education, and assessment. We hope you join us in creating the physical education classroom of the future!

Acknowledgments

We wish to thank so many people. First, we would like to thank the Saint Mary's University students in Dan Midura's and Don Glover's Team Building classes for providing us with so many excellent team builders over the last 10 years. Thank you to Carol Glover for babysitting Jake and Josh so the authors could meet and write. Thank you to the students in PE 326 at the University of Wisconsin—River Falls. These students truly are going to be the best teachers in the world! We would especially like to thank the following students from that class—Katie Bernardy, Kacey Hilgendorf, Jenny Tweet, Amy Ward, Molly Dressen, Aaron Bayer, Matt Roerig, and Tony Olson for some of the ideas in this book

We also want to thank Brooke Kieper for her excellent typing skills; the Gopher employees who value and exhibit the lessons being taught in this book; and physical education teachers Cheryl Fregeau, Jennifer Younquist, Roxy Myhre, Jeff Casey. These teachers are pioneers in their districts in the area of portfolios as a means to assess their students. They are risk takers, advocates for change, and have provided many ideas and activities in the assessment chapter. We would also like to thank Cindy Stevenson for her inspiration, guidance, and time she provided in the area of brain research and Kari Dahl for sharing her wealth of knowledge and talents in the area of assessment.

We would especially like to thank the wonderful staff in the Health and Human Performance Department at the University of Wisconsin—River Falls and Saint Mary's University. These instructors are creating the best teaching product anywhere and you make us proud to be part of your working communities. Thanks to Joyce Locks, former physical education professor at Winona State University, for her inspiration.

Finally, thanks to Jennifer Walker, our developmental editor, for her patience, thoughtful questioning, and guidance with this project.

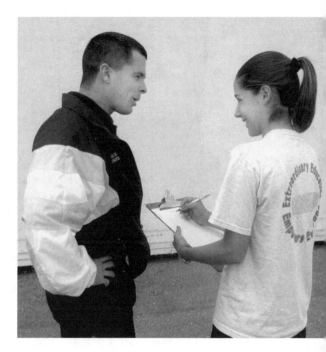

Brain Research and Competition in Physical Education

In this chapter, we introduce the positive and negative influences physical education and competition can have on students. Specifically, we address the following:

- How brain research relates to physical education
- How threatening situations in physical education turn kids away from fitness
- Why the emotional needs of students must be met before significant learning can occur or connections can be made
- What harmful effects competition can have on children

Key Terms
- Brain research
- Emotional intelligence
- Threat
- Harmful competition
- Effective competition

Teachers who choose to teach physical education often do so because it has always been of particular interest to them. Many of them were (or are) athletes, and many of them simply enjoy fitness. Naturally, they will be better equipped to connect with and understand students who have similar interests. What PE teacher isn't excited when he or she discovers a natural athlete in class? It's probably a bit more difficult for the PE instructors to relate to the students who hate to run or cannot catch a ball if their life depended on it. Noted business speaker and motivational expert Stephen Covey (1989) illustrates a concept of "seeking first to understand," and this philosophy has great importance in the PE setting. He states how important it is for the teacher to truly understand students individually before motivation can take place.

For example, think back to how many times we have wondered why we can't get students to understand us? In comparison, how many times have we attempted to truly understand our students and what they find motivating? Covey says that to develop positive relationships, we need to understand other people before we can expect them to understand us. This concept is pivotal to our tapping into students' intrinsic motivation to learn. We must understand the needs and the beliefs of our students as they are, not as we think that they ought to be (Rogers and Renard 1999). One of the best ways to understand the needs and benefits of students is to start on the inside—specifically, we must start with their minds and how they work.

Brain Research and the New Physical Education

Brain research has influenced education tremendously in the last few years. In fact, the 1990s were declared by President George Bush as the "decade of the brain." This focus on understanding the inner workings of student behaviors and motivations has carried on into the 21st century, largely because of the wave of information from research. This new information allows educators to make major strides in constructing their physical classrooms and their learning styles in a way that is more "brain compatible." Programs that promote community and a sense of belonging among all participants are slowly taking over classrooms across America, and the results are proving very beneficial. Additionally, character education and team building are innovative strategies that focus on community and character building. They create a positive influence in teaching kids to be good competitors, and they help make an emotionally supportive environment that is crucial to learning. Adding to the mix of friendlier instructional strategies is portfolio assessment, a new form of assessment that allows learners to take more ownership in their learning, which in turn increases their intrinsic motivation. As a whole, community-based learning programs, character education and team building, and portfolio assessment genuinely create a completely new breed of physical education.

In fact, all of these programs, although somewhat new to education, have had an overwhelmingly positive influence. One of the reasons these programs are so beneficial, and are thus becoming as popular as they are, is that they support what experts say about how the brain actually learns. The issue in this book, however, is not to explore how successful these programs have been in regular education but rather what they mean to physical education and how they can be incorporated.

Physical Education and Threats

In the various discussions we've had with adults, adolescents, and children regarding physical education, we've found that many of their experiences were positive. For example, a high percentage of students in elementary school claim physical education to be their favorite class. However, through these discussions, we also learned that physical education can also be a very threatening place. It not only can be difficult for students physically, it can be one of the most emotionally stressful classes in school. In fact, many of the current practices in physical education classes go against what researchers and educators now say are the optimal ways to learn. Why then is it so popular among students? Is it one of the favorite classes in school, or is that maybe an assumption that many of us have?

First of all, think about the mind-set and social pressures of children today—specifically, those related to physical education. It's simply not cool for a middle school boy to not like sports when our society glamorizes them so much. More than likely, he would keep his opinions quiet or risk being ridiculed and ostracized by his peers. In addition, we've learned through interviews and experience that students in kindergarten through fifth grade often say physical education is their favorite class, but that changes immensely as kids grow older. Why do many kids begin their years in school loving physical education and slowly change that attitude as they enter into the intermediate and middle school years? Could it be that the stakes begin to get higher as testing becomes more common and the will to win becomes more intense?

The importance of learning in community and eliminating the threat of an educational setting go hand in hand, and they are continually stressed as we learn more about the brain. Learning and emotion simply cannot be separated. One's emotional needs must be met if the maximum amount of learning is to take place. However, in spite of mounting evidence, this issue is often not stressed in teacher education programs—especially physical education programs—and many educators believe that tending to the emotional needs of a student is simply "fluff" and a waste of time.

Noted brain researcher Daniel Goldman (1997) states in his book *Emotional Intelligence* that 20 percent of success is determined by IQ (intelligence quotient) and 80 percent of success is determined by EQ (emotional quotient). According to Goldman, "Emotional intelligence includes self-awareness and impulse control, persistence, zeal and self-motivation, empathy and social deftness. These are the qualities that mark people who excel in real life: whose intimate relationships flourish, who are the stars in the workplace. These are also the hallmarks of character and self-discipline, of altruism and compassion—basic capacities needed in our society to thrive." In his book, he examines the factors when people of high IQ flounder and those of modest IQ do surprisingly well. Goldman's work, with all of the other brain research that supports it, indicates that meeting the emotional needs of students is key to motivation and learning.

Likewise, memory is also directly correlated with emotions. Goldman states that situations and experiences that include emotional arousal are imprinted in our memory with an added degree of strength: "That's why we are more likely, for example, to remember where we went on a first date, or what we were doing when we heard the news that the space shuttle Challenger had exploded. The more intense the . . . arousal, the stronger the imprint; the experiences that scare or thrill us the most in life are among our most indelible."

If you think back to some of your most memorable experiences from kindergarten to 12th grade, an emotion is more than likely to be tied to that memory. In other words, you can probably remember how you felt in those situations. Think back to some of your favorite teachers. Do you remember how you felt being around them or in their classroom? How about the teachers you disliked the most? What was the strongest emotion when you entered their classroom?

In the book *10 Best Teaching Practices* (2000), Donna Walker Tileston writes:

> The evidence is so overwhelming that an enriched and emotionally supportive environment is necessary if students and faculty are to grow mentally that to ignore this aspect of education should be considered malpractice. Thirty-plus years of research say that not just rats, but children, thrive in this environment. Perhaps today more than at any other time in history we need to provide an environment for students that is stress reduced and has as its central goal to be a place to belong. That means that all gifts are valued and that every student has an opportunity to learn without fear of being embarrassed or excluded. Teachers must begin to view themselves as partners in the learning, as catalysts for the classroom, not the center of the learning. An enriched environment has less to do with posters on the wall and more to do with challenging, stimulating, and fun activities that tantalize the thought processes, raise the oxygen level in the brain, and cause people to want to be there. If we cannot create a climate in which all students feel physically and emotionally secure, the rest doesn't matter.

Biology and Threat

Of great value to PE teachers is the research related to learning and threat, which shows that the brain operates differently when it feels threatened. When people feel threatened in any way, it means that they are experiencing negative stress and that their emotions are running high. The limbic system, also known as the *midbrain,* is the part of the brain that controls emotion. Anatomically, the limbic system is wrapped around the top of the brain stem, between the brain stem and the neocortex (the intellectual part of the brain that controls the higher-order thinking skills, such as logic and reasoning). Blood has to flow through the limbic system to get to the neocortex. When a person's emotions are being threatened or when there is any type of negative stress, the blood flow through the limbic system decreases—thus, limiting the amount of blood that reaches the "thinking brain" (the neocortex). This means that there is limited activity and that it can't function to its capacity. Jensen (2000) describes it this way: "The limbic system is often referred to as the guardian at the gate—the guardian of emotions at the gate of intellect. Emotions are seen as the gateway to the thinking mind. If the emotional guard is up, very little cognitive reasoning is likely to occur. The emotions rule over reason and thinking is often blurred when emotions are high."

When threat decreases blood flow and limits activity in the neocortex, there is an increase in blood flow to the brain stem, which is actually often referred to as the "reptilian brain." This part of the brain controls the survival behaviors instinctive to an infant, often characterized as the "fight-or-flight behaviors." In a negative situation, such as being embarrassed by coming in last place or feeling angry after being put down or yelled at, students might fight to get out of that situation. As a result, they may often demonstrate the negative behaviors we see in students (the "fight" response), or they may withdraw and retreat from the situation (the "flight response"). Unfulfilled needs often lead to destructive behaviors (Schneider 1996). Oftentimes these behaviors are controlled by the brain stem because the thinking part of the brain isn't functioning to capacity. The following quote just may provide some insight as to why some students continually display negative behaviors in class: "Sometimes the kids who are hardest to love are the ones that need it the most."

Regardless, we punish students with undesirable behavior in many situations when instead we need to try to understand them so that we can best meet their needs. Negative behaviors can often be eliminated when the student is in an environment where they feel valued, safe, and involved in activities that are meaningful to them.

Tileston (2000) gives further insight on this subject: "Students who feel threatened in the classroom, whether physically or emotionally, are operating in a survival mode, and while learning can take place in that mode, it is with much difficulty. If a student feels that no matter how hard he/she tries they can never understand the subject—whether the threat is real or perceived—he/she will not ever be able to reach his potential in that environment."

Threatening situations may take on many different forms, with physical threat being the most obvious. However, intellectual, emotional, and social threats can be equally as harmful on learning and motivation, and they often go unnoticed. Jensen (2000) again gives some examples of types of threats.

Potential Physical Harm

- From classmates, staff, family, others

Intellectual Threats

- A test or essay returned with derisive comments
- Lack of information to meet the task requirements
- Inconsistency in grading

Emotional Threats

- Potentially embarrassing moments

- Put-downs or sarcasm
- Reward systems that threaten withdrawal if not achieved
- Lack of understanding about limits or expectations

Cultural-Social Threats
- Isolated from peers, working by oneself
- Unable to pursue personal values at school
- Limited chance to utilize meaningful personal life

The following is how they relate specifically to physical education.

Potential Physical Harm

- From classmates, staff, family, others

Could students feel physically threatened in physical education? Have we ever asked? Besides recess and situations before and after school, physical education would probably be the most obvious place where students may worry about getting physically harmed. Most students probably don't feel threatened in this capacity, especially the more active and athletic; however, physical education classes serve more than just the athletic students. How do we know the answer if we don't address the situation and try to eliminate that threat, if in fact it does exist?

We've all seen children cower in fear as a ball comes speeding toward them or a timid child quietly move out of the way as another drives in full speed for a layup. Many times these children are written off as "wimpy" or nonaggressive, when instead we need to realize that just as not all students have an interest in music, not all children have an interest in athletics either. Our goal for those children should be to help them develop an interest in fitness so that they will want to continue to exercise throughout their lives. We need to provide alternatives for them so that they can figure out what they are most interested in. Competitive games aren't for everyone, and they generate fear in several ways for many.

Kari and Physical Threat

Kari, a college professor, loathes sports and physical fitness altogether: "In school, I hated PE because I was always afraid I was going to get hurt. I had to play these games, and the boys would always throw the ball so hard. I never could understand why I had to play trench ball when I hated it so much."

It would be much more powerful if students had a choice in how they wanted to improve their individual skills or, more important, how they were going to exercise to stay healthy. Isn't that the underlying goal of physical education anyway, helping people develop an appreciation for physical fitness so that they can maintain a healthy lifestyle? The power of choice in one's learning has taken off in regular-education settings, but not so much in physical education.

Choice and Physical Education

A very common theme in providing a brain-friendly environment is for students to have a say in how they learn and even what they learn. Traditionally, this hasn't been an option as the teacher stood up front and dictated. What was important and meaningful to the student often was not considered, and, as a result, students participated in activities that had no impact. They became very dependant on the teacher to spoon-feed information while they went through the motions of learning. If our ultimate goal is to encourage lifelong participation in activity then the students should start making choices at the elementary level.

In the classroom, we empower students when we involve them in the class rules and when we give them choices in the assignments. As a matter of fact, any time we give students choices, we give them power (Tileston 2000), and when a student feels empowered they feel cared for and validated. When we provide choices we are celebrating individuality and increasing self-motivation as students are allowed to partake in activities that are meaningful to them.

Providing choices is not only a key factor in helping students celebrate their strengths, it's a determining factor on whether a student is going to learn and become intrinsically motivated in the subject matter. If students know they have a say in what they participate in or how they are going to meet an objective, chances are they are going to want to be there and have an invested interest in learning and striving for goals.

Intellectual Threats (Attacks on One's Ideas or Potential)

- A test or essay returned with derisive comments
- Lack of information to meet the task requirements
- Inconsistency in grading

Intellectual threats can also be very common in physical education. For example, students are often expected to remember drills or rules to games.

What happens if they don't? Are they yelled at, which is often what happens with the drill-sergeant approach? Are they graded down on a written test? Or, are they encouraged in a safe environment to ask the teacher questions or, better yet, their classmates?

Portfolio assessment can easily eliminate this form of threat, with students striving toward goals they have set for themselves. Being graded can often feel threatening, especially when expectations aren't always clear. Sometimes students are graded solely on ability, which means that the athletic get As and the unathletic get Cs. Many teachers combine work ethic, attitude, and ability while considering each grade. This, of course, seems much better and a lot fairer, but how can we expect the students who are uncoordinated and continually embarrassed in front of their peers to maintain a positive attitude?

Emotional Threats (Feelings or Self-Esteem Criticized)

- Potentially embarrassing moments
- Put-downs or sarcasm
- Reward systems that threaten withdrawal if not achieved
- Lack of understanding about limits or expectations

Emotional threats are probably the most common types of threats in physical education. The risk of embarrassment is a fear many have in the gym. They may be embarrassed because they are the last one picked for a team, or they may dread going up to bat because they feel like they're going to strike out anyway. Situations like this may not be obvious, but for those students who may not be quite as athletic or for the more and more who are now overweight, they are going to do anything they can to not be noticed. Kari, the woman mentioned earlier, has nothing but bad memories about physical education: "I was much uncoordinated and was terrible at everything. It was humiliating because I had to do what everyone else had to do, and the whole class could see how bad I was. Those group tests were the worst. I remember having to do pull-ups with everyone watching, and I couldn't even do one. I was so embarrassed."

Kari has an 11-year-old daughter who is now experiencing some of the same frustrations. "Unfortunately, she has been blessed with my athletic ability, and she also feels humiliated at times. On the day of the track-and-field testing, I wrote a note excusing her from school, saying she was sick, so she wouldn't have to do those worthless tests. I just don't see the point. My daughter loves music—why couldn't she do something like dance for exercise instead of those competitive games and fitness tests?"

Obviously, Kari and her daughter have experienced a lot of negative stress in physical education. When asked if her behavior changed in physical education, Kari answered with a definite *yes.* "I am an extroverted individual, and I always was one to speak up in my classes. However, in physical education, I withdrew and did anything I could not to be noticed."

What is the point of fitness tests that are often set up for the whole class to watch? Are the out-of-shape children who struggle in the mile-run going to get turned on to fitness through embarrassment? Is the uncoordinated boy who continually strikes out when he's up to bat going to be excited about playing baseball in the future? Probably not. Chances are that those students are only going to dislike athletics more.

One of the many problems with competitive games is the amount of put-downs that take place among participants. If put-downs are tolerated, positive progress is simply not going to be made. Many regular-education teachers do not like teaching physical education because of how the students treat each other. Competition often brings out the more negative characteristics in many children, especially when the "win at all costs" attitude has been modeled by the adults in their lives—which is precisely the reason why character education and team building should be implemented into the physical education curriculum. In fact, it's probably the most natural fit because it is the class where your character is most likely to be tested. The following chapters go into detail about how to build character in your students to help eliminate the negative behaviors that often result from competitive situations, and describe how to become a good teammate and respectful competitor.

Cultural-Social Threats (Disrespect)

- Isolated from peers, working by oneself
- Unable to pursue personal values at school
- Limited chance to utilize meaningful personal life

Parker Palmer, a highly respected educational author, states that our images of reality have gone from fragmentation and competition to community and collaboration. This change has gone right along with the scientific evidence that shows how we learn best. In many cases, education has moved right along with this transformation, stressing the importance of cooperative learning in the classroom. This transformation should be no different in physical education. Students should view their classmates as collaborators in learning, rather than competitors in the quest for grades and recognition (Schaps, Lewis, and Watson 1996). Because physical education and sports are related, competition is naturally going to be part of the curriculum. From day one, students need to be taught the importance of working together, and it needs to be stressed and modeled religiously throughout the year. Students, teachers, parents, and coaches need to have ingrained in their minds that for teams to reach their maximum potential, every member needs to feel valued and committed to one another's growth. In addition, it can't be assumed that students know how to be good team members. Teamwork has to be taught and continually stressed throughout the year. Team building through physical challenges has been a way to incorporate and stress the importance of teamwork, and it's been a positive change from competitive games in that it can increase self-esteem among all participants—not just the ones who score the most points.

Alfie Kohn, author of No Contest (1992) and Punishment by Rewards (1993), writes, "You can't build self-esteem unless you are doing something for or with others." People of all ages have benefited and thoroughly enjoyed the camaraderie that results when participating in team-building activities.

Being successful is key in becoming and remaining intrinsically motivated. Students need to see progress being made, and they need to experience the gratification of accomplishing a goal that is meaningful to them. This can be tough to do when students have no idea what the goal is or when the goal is imposed on them by someone else. For example, Kari didn't like playing trench ball because she got absolutely nothing out of it. To this day, she still has no idea why she had to play games like that when she didn't enjoy them and when they scared her so much. Likewise, if students have no say in what the particular goal is, it may not be as meaningful to them, and therefore, striving toward it may not be as important. Chapter 4 provides suggestions on how to make specific units valuable for all students, as we go in depth on the use of portfolios in physical education.

Remember what we said earlier about teachers who choose to teach physical education because it is of particular interest to them and more than likely always has been? Remember how we said that they're naturally going to connect with and understand students who have similar interests and that it's probably more difficult for them to relate to students who don't care for athletic endeavors, such as sports and exercise. Consider again Stephen Covey's concept of "seeking first to understand" and how it states the value of the teacher's true understanding of each student individually before any intrinsic motivation can take place.

Let's revisit our friend Kari. Maybe Kari would have a different attitude toward physical fitness and sports if someone had taken the time to understand what she wanted or taken the time to help her with specific skills. She states, "One of my best friends is a PE teacher and a former stand-out fast-pitch softball pitcher. Once in awhile, she tries to teach me how to pitch. It makes such a difference when she tells me specifically what I am doing right and what I am doing wrong. I feel so much more successful because I realize that I can do athletic activities, especially when someone takes the time to help me on the specific skills. I actually kind of enjoy it."

Competition and Threat

Probably the two most threatening situations that take place in physical education are competitive situations and assessment. We take a much deeper look at assessment in chapter 4, but for this chapter, we'd like to remain focused on competition. Because competition is so prevalent in physical education, we want to discuss how it can be used more productively. Competitive situations go against the brain research that has positively influenced many of our schools today. In fact, many researchers are saying that competition is harmful and doesn't even belong in our schools. However, we believe that when used effectively, *competition does have a place in physical education and can produce positive results.* Chapters 2 and 3 provide specific hands-on activities that teach kids how to be respectful competitors as well as how to turn negative competitive situations into positive learning experiences.

Defining Competition

Competition in itself encompasses every type of threat we have already discussed in this chapter. When I was a sixth-grade regular-ed teacher, I did my master's thesis on incorporating teamwork into competitive situations. I quickly learned that competition can be very disturbing, and it often causes more harm than good. When I started my thesis project, I asked a number of regular-ed elementary teachers what the biggest reason was regarding why they didn't like teaching physical education. The responses fell into three categories, one major and two minor: 73 percent said it was the way the students treated each other, the fighting and the put-downs; 13 percent said there was too much complaining; and another 13 percent said it was that the students don't listen. Many of these teachers also mentioned that they often just let the students have free time on the playground during PE time because playing organized games was too stressful.

I have a strong physical education and coaching background and have always loved sports, but I, too, started to dread teaching physical education. It was so frustrating seeing the negative behaviors that often surfaced in the gym. Bad attitudes started in a few and spread quickly, and many students were simply not having any fun. They spent most of their 30 minutes of gym time fighting or complaining. What was very bewildering was that I had a great class, full of very nice kids! It eventually made no sense to me to even go to physical education anymore, as everyone left the gym mad, including me. The thing that surprised me the most about competitive situations was not how they treated their opponents, but how they treated their own teammates.

I started becoming much more aware of the students' attitudes once they stepped into the gym. What was very interesting was that the behaviors not only changed when they were in physical education, but also in any type of competitive situation. I soon realized that competitive games could really bring out the negative qualities in people. I began to key in on some individuals who had the most problems in competitive situations. Tim, who was very big and strong, couldn't hold back tears when things didn't go his way. Peter had a very bad temper and often lost it in the heat of the battle. And finally, Jesse, who happened to be one of my most well-behaved boys in the classroom, continually complained about things not being fair. I decided to look into some of their sports backgrounds outside of school.

Each of the boys played football and hockey, and they happened to be on the same teams. I called the parents of the boy who had the most trouble and told his mom I was concerned about how her son would lose his temper when he gets upset. I then gave some specific examples of situations in the gym, as well as in the classroom. Without even asking, she volunteered information about the coach of his hockey team. She seemed sure these attitudes were coming from his coach. His philosophy about sports was basically, "Do what you need to do to win." He also encouraged the boys to "fight" if they needed to and "never back down." She sounded very concerned as she was telling me this, and she didn't seem to know what to do. I then asked about the other adults in his life who supported his athletics. She explained that his football coach had a similar philosophy but wasn't quite as hard on the boys. We ended the conversation with some ideas on how we could help him change his behavior.

As a result of the behaviors I was seeing and the conflict that resulted, I started choosing more activities that weren't as competitive. I soon realized, however, that I was avoiding something that will always be a big part of their lives. What I ultimately learned was that physical education is the optimal place to help give them the tools they need to be respectful competitors and turn competitive situations into growing experiences.

For example, in the professional world, teamwork is a very important characteristic to have to be successful. If one of our jobs as educators is to prepare our students with skills that will help them be successful in the future, then why isn't teamwork considered a crucial part of curriculums? With this in mind, I decided to no longer get angry and frustrated at the way students treated each other in competitive situations. This approach was simply not doing them any good. They needed to be taught the characteristics of being a good teammate; they did not need to be scolded for lack of knowing them. Then, they needed to be given the opportunities to practice their newly learned skills. As a result, we now view competitive situations as opportunities to enhance abilities to be good teammates as well as develop good sporting behavior.

Harmful vs. Effective Competition

To some, competition is regarded as natural, healthy, and essential for building character. They say it is a valuable means to socialize children, a significant force in motivating behavior, and highly enjoyable. To others, competition is regarded as harmful, psychologically injurious, and detrimental to cooperative activity. It is declared as being destructive, irrational, and highly counterproductive (Martens 1977). These are obviously very opposing views. We believe that competition can be both productive and counterproductive and that it's the adults or role models who can determine what effects competition can have on a child.

Despite beliefs that competitive sport is harmful to children, one thing is very clear: Competition is a big part of our children's lives, and it's here to stay for a long time. With that in mind, whether we like it or not, we have to make the most of it to create positive experiences for our children. Little League and other community and commercially sponsored sports are taking up many families' weekends, with games now being played even on Sundays. There are more opportunities than ever for children to participate in organized sport. As a result, coaches are in short supply. Parents who volunteer to coach often have no experience working with children. Unfortunately, many of these volunteers pressure children to win, in which case competition becomes destructive. With so many outside negative forces, physical educators are fighting an uphill battle when they try to stress the importance of teamwork.

What is wrong with competition today is the attitude "Winning isn't everything, it's the only thing," as stated by Vince Lombardi. This illustrates a destructive model of competition and why many researchers have claimed competition harmful. According to James Michener (1976) in *Sports in America*, Lombardi even regretted saying this. He retracted the statement shortly before he died, saying that he had meant putting forth the effort necessary to win was important, not stamping out values and morality in order to win. Unfortunately, many adults still do have this attitude and are passing it on to children at a high expense. The following letters give examples of harmful competition and the effects it can have on the people involved.

Dear Mom and Dad

Letter appeared in *You and Your Child in Hockey*, 1975.

Dear Mom and Dad,

I hope that you won't get mad at me for writing this letter, but you always told me never to keep anything back that ought to be brought out into the open. So here goes.

Remember the other morning when my team was playing and both of you were sitting and watching? Well, I hope that you won't get mad at me, but you kind of embarrassed me. Remember when I went after the puck in front of the net trying to score and fell? I could hear you yelling at the goalie for getting in my way and tripping me. It wasn't his fault that is what he is supposed to do. Then do you remember yelling at me to get on the other side of the blue line? The coach told me to cover my man, and I couldn't if I listened to you, and while I tried to decide they scored against us. Then you yelled at me for being in the wrong place. You shouldn't have jumped all over the coach for pulling me off the ice. He is a pretty good coach, and a good guy, and he knows what he is doing. Besides he is just a volunteer coming down all hours of the day helping us kids, just because he loves the sport. And, then neither of you spoke to me the whole way home; I guess I am a crummy hockey player. But, I love the game; it is lots of fun being with . . .

What's This World Coming To?

By Nik Pfaffinger, young soccer player in Kitchenere, Ontario. Letter to the editor, which appeared in the *Kitchener-Waterloo Record*, June 19, 1976.

To the Editor:

Although I am only 12 years old I can tell poor sportsmanship when I see it. Not among young people like myself but among adults.

On June 16 our team (Laurentian Acadians) was playing the Rockway team. With four minutes left to play and the score 1-0 in our favor a Rockway boy kicked the ball down the sideline. I and most people thought it went out, and the ref called it that way. Suddenly a Rockway father jumped out on the pitch and started to hassle the ref. After a great deal of arguing the man hit the ref. When the ref walked away the man spit at him. After the game the man punched the ref again. He hassled the ref all the way to his car.

We have had many similar experiences and it ruins the game. It must be very frustrating for the referees who are only trying to do their best.

My friends and I play soccer for the fun of it, and we wonder, what is the world coming to?

Let the Kids Play

By Hall Lebovitz, sports editor for the *Cleveland Plain Dealer*.

After four unforgettable years my son and I have ended our Little League careers, he as a player, I as a spectator. This is my valedictory, written in the hope that other fathers and, yes, even mothers, may see the light.

Frankly, I thought my behavior at the games was exemplary and adult. But recently I decided to interview my son. For years I have been interviewing the Yogi Berras, the Ted Williams, the Jimmy Browns, and the Jack Dempseys. Why not Neil Lebovitz my favorite Little League catcher?

"Are you enjoying Little League ball?" I asked him.

"Yes, dad, a lot."

"Is there anything I could do to help make it more enjoyable?"

"Well, dad, you know a lot about baseball, probably more than most fathers . . ."

My chest expanded several inches until he said, "But . . ." This one word punctured the balloon completely.

"But," he continued, "I wish you wouldn't talk to me during the game. You keep yelling at me, 'Get up closer,' and 'Don't step away,' and things like that. I try to listen to you and the manager and watch the ball all at the same time and I don't feel comfortable. It gets me confused."

"Well, I'm only trying to help."

"I know," he said. "But you asked me, dad, so I'm telling you. If you want to help me improve, I'd like it better if you waited until we got home."

"Is there anything I could say at the game—if I had to say something—that would help you?"

"Well, I like it when my teammates tell me, 'Don't worry, you'll get 'em next time,' after I do something wrong. I like it when you compliment me and encourage me. I don't like it when you tell me what I'm doing wrong at the game."

So ended our interview. Needless to say I was jarred. But I knew he was right. He was saying "Let me play my own game. You can't play it for me." He was reminding me of the truism "Build! Don't belittle," or phrased more commonly, "Boost! Don't Knock."

It was no consolation to me to know that I was no different from other fathers. I discussed the matter with George Kell, former major league great who is now broadcasting the Tigers' games. He too, has a Little League son.

"When my boy takes a third strike it kills me," he confessed. "When he gets a hit I'm reborn. More so than when I experienced those things myself. It's funny how we blow up at our kid's mistakes, forgetting that we made them ourselves. You'd think I never took a third strike or dropped a ball."

The ultimate danger of our actions was revealed by George McKinnon, the baseball coach at Cleveland Heights High. "In our community we have a marvelous Little League program," he said. "You'd think we'd eventually get a lot of talent from it for our high school team. But by the time the boys reach us most of them have turned to other interests. And do your know the reason? Their parents made baseball so frustrating they turned to something in which there was less parental pressure."

Still, I'm delighted my boy played Little League ball. Sports opens doors to friendships as no other endeavor can. I'm especially glad we had that father-son interview, late as it was. During the final weeks of the season he played his own game. I stopped playing it for him. He was a much better player. Clearly, he had more fun. Surprisingly, so did I.

Unfortunately, these letters illustrate how a high percentage of our youth feel on a daily basis. We need to take into consideration the outside forces that affect so many students. We need to continually think of ways to make competition a fun, productive, nonthreatening activity in which students genuinely want to participate.

The following descriptions outline different forms of competition. The Military Model illustrates harmful competition, and the Partnership Model describes the direction we need to go to avoid driving so many kids away from sports at such an early age.

Military Model of Competition

These attitudes of competition are detrimental to a child's development, and unfortunately, they are quite common. "These adult corrupted activities teach kids how to fight and cheat, they exclude those who could benefit most, and they cripple and maim the young in the pursuit of victory"

(Martin Ralbovsky 1974). In interviewing several students, we found that the top reasons students participate in athletics are to have fun, make friends, and stay in shape. Winning was near the bottom. The problem exists, however, when the coach's priorities are the opposite, with winning being at the top. Of course, all coaches should want to win, and it should definitely be something to shoot for, but many take it much more seriously at the expense of the athletes they are coaching. What many coaches don't realize is that if they were to make developing relationships and meeting the emotional needs of their athletes a top priority, winning will be much more likely to occur. For more information on the Military Model of Competition see *The Competition-Cooperation Link* (Midura and Glover 1999, page 6).

Partnership Model of Competition

In contrast to the military model is the Partnership Model of Competition. It emphasizes that teammates, coaches, and even opposing players view each other as comrades rather than enemies. Players with disparate ability levels are respected as peers rather than ranked hierarchy, and athletes care for each other and their bodies.

Chris, 35 years old, was an excellent athlete in high school and still is very active in physical fitness. "Sports were and still are a huge part of my life. I grew up competing on organized teams, and I look back at them as being some of the most positive experiences of my life. My parents were very supportive and their attitude was, as sportswriter Grantland Rice once said, 'It's not whether you win or lose, it's how you play the game.' I feel my toughest opponent in competition was myself. I always strived to improve and reach the goal I set. I also met some of my best friends on the teams I played on, and against. One of the many reasons I looked forward to going to practice every day was the camaraderie amongst my teammates."

Like early physical educators, partnership athletes maintain that sport should be inclusive, in balance with other aspects of life, cooperative and social in spirit, and safe (Oglesby 1989). To learn more about the Partnership Model of Competition see *The Competition-Cooperation Link* (Midura and Glover 1999, page 7).

Reward Model of Competition

Most scientists and scholars who have studied competition, including Alfie Kohn (1992), define competition by the "reward definition," which simply means that everyone who competes is doing so for the same reason—winning. In this model of competition, it is assumed that everyone who is competing does so to beat the other competitors. The reward definition is an inadequate way to describe competition because it is difficult or impossible to achieve consensus on what the goals are for each individual or team competing. Thus, each individual or team may have a different definition of what their reward may be in going out for athletics.

For example, athletes often enjoy playing better-skilled athletes because it helps raise their own skill level. Kim, a former high school standout, explains it like this: "When I was a sophomore in high school, I loved playing one-on-one against the all-state guard on my basketball team. I knew I would have very little chance in beating her, but I felt like my level of play rose when playing her because I had to work so much harder to get a basket or prevent her from getting one." Kim didn't look at her opponent as an object getting in the way of her success, but rather a teammate contributing to her improvement. In addition, the two happen to be very good friends. In a similar situation, Mark was an average tennis player who had the opportunity to play the club pro at the health club where he worked out: "My goal is not to win; my goal is to not embarrass myself too bad and play reasonably well." It is clear that Mark's goal and the reward he seeks are quite different than his opponent's. Thus, defining competition on the basis of rewards or winning makes little sense because the rewards are subjectively determined (Martens 1977).

For more on Reward Model of Competition see *The Competition-Cooperation Link* (Midura and Glover 1999, page 6). Whether they want it or not, competitive activities are a large part of the lives of our youth. The modeling and attitudes of the parents, coaches, teachers, and other adults in their lives are pivotal in determining if these situations will make or break a child. Physical education can play a big role in influencing not only the attitudes of the students involved but of their parents and coaches as well. Fortunately, physical educators are in an influential position, and they need to spread the word about what is best for our kids. We can't afford the statistics to get any worse.

The attitude toward competition is just one of the many factors in physical education that are turning kids away. Lack of choice and meaningless goals are also contributing factors, but perhaps the most detrimental aspect of physical education today is that we are forgetting about the emotional needs of our students. Creating a safe, welcoming atmosphere in which all kids feel significant, regardless of their athletic ability, could make a huge difference in the health and well-being of our society and attitudes toward fitness.

As stated throughout this chapter, students cannot establish an emotional connection to physical education if they feel excluded or threatened in any way. The following chapters are going to give you hands-on activities and strategies to make physical education a positive, brain-friendly place for everyone!

Motivators, Huddles, and Warm-Ups

If we cannot create a climate in which all students feel physically and emotionally secure, the rest doesn't matter.

Tileston, 2000

A Sense of Belonging

All of us want to belong somewhere. We want to feel we are part of the experience and that we are accepted. When students do not feel accepted, for whatever reason, they are more likely to find negative places to belong. This lack of acceptance is what helps to keep gangs active in our students' lives. Gangs and other negative influences fill a need that so often is not met in positive settings. As educators we must create an environment in which students feel safe and accepted, an environment in which we are all learners together and where we feel a sense of togetherness—one where there are no "gotchas."

Tileston, 2000

This chapter is the heart and soul of this book. It provides hands-on activities to help create an environment in which everyone feels they belong and are a significant part of the class. This chapter focuses on creating a ritual at the beginning of each class period that creates a friendly and welcoming atmosphere, promotes social relationships, builds character, empowers students, and makes learning and exercise fun!

This ritual consists of three components. First, the motivator. The motivator ensures that each student gets recognized upon entering class. The second component is the huddle, which consists of character-building discussion activities. The last component of this ritual is the warm-up. These warm-ups are unique in that they not only warm up the body for exercise, but they build community as well. By incorporating this ritual into your class on a regular basis, you will be on your way to an environment where students will want to be, where they will want to learn, and where they will be fired up to exercise! In this chapter, you will learn the following:

- How to incorporate a ritual at the beginning of each class period
- How to set up a class that promotes security and a sense of belonging among students
- How to incorporate character education and conflict-resolution skills into your program
- How to eliminate the fears students have while participating in physical education and replace those feelings with a sense of empowerment and excitement
- How to build community, how to warm up for class, and how to have fun—all at the same time, with the 28 team warm-up ideas given

Key Terms
- Motivators
- Huddles
- Warm-ups
- Character education

- Fitness buddies
- Team talks

Teams—A New Way to Start Class

Upon entering the gym, students traditionally report to their squads. The squads are usually in a straight line and are convenient for the teacher. This method facilitates taking roll and organizing for exercises.

Another traditional method for organizing a physical education class is for the students to count off by fours. As the students enter the gym, they stand on the black line. When everyone is present they count off. All the number 4s take eight steps forward; the number 3s take six steps; the number 2s take four steps; and the number 1s stay on the line. Again, all the students are organized for activity and separated into teams.

Many elementary physical education teachers start class with, "Come into the gym, find your own space, and sit down." Then they give the warm-up and instructions for the day. Other physical education classes have no specific setup; students simply enter the gym and stand around until given instruction. With this format, students get with their friends and chat until class begins, but there are always students standing by themselves, feeling left out.

All of these methods have been shown to work when the main focus is exercising or organization, but they are impersonal. They do nothing to foster communication or the feeling of belonging to a group or team. In fact, each method actually fosters isolation.

Now, what we are proposing is a new way to start class: "Report directly to your teams." The reason for this is to have a safety net for the students immediately upon their entering the gym. We feel that teachers can create a safer, friendly atmosphere when they establish a smaller group setting and have students report directly to their teams.

Research has shown that a crucial step in creating an ideal learning environment is to begin class with a group of people with whom students feel comfortable and accepted. The more students know and trust those around them, the more willing they are to open themselves up and take risks. Once the teacher has decided upon the makeup of the teams, students should be instructed to report directly to their teams at the beginning of class and sit in a circle, as this facilitates communication and group spirit. Everyone can make eye contact, and it simply creates a more welcoming atmosphere.

After the third or fourth week of school, this ritual becomes routine without the teacher having to instruct students. Together, these teams participate in many activities that build character, as well as community. At the beginning of the year, teams should be responsible for the following.

- Team name: Keep them positive!
- Team handshake: Teams need to come up with a special handshake, unique to their team, and it can include any nontraditional way to shake another person's hand.
- Team break or cheer: This could be as simple as everyone putting their hands on top of one another's in a group huddle and on the count of three, yelling the team name. Or, it could be as involved and as creative as teams want it to be. We asked college students to come up with a team handshake, not really knowing how involved it would get. We were pleasantly surprised when many of them created routines that they were very excited about.

If the teacher has any examples of sports teams doing fancy handshakes or cheers, they should show them to the students to give them an idea of what they are. Athletes from the high school could also be invited to model what their team does as a special cheer or handshake. We discuss more of this later in the chapter.

Elementary students could spend a bit more time coming up with their special cheer in other classes. It would be a great activity to do in language arts or dramatics class, and it's a fantastic way to connect physical education with different subjects. It fits in well with other disciplines because it allows for creativity in many ways. Working on this cheer, however, for middle school and high school students would have to be in the physical education setting, as they often don't see each other in other classes. As a result, their team cheer or break would be less involved and much shorter.

Team Setup

We encourage that six to eight students be on a team. Each student is to be assigned a number, determined by the number of students on the team. For example, on a team of six, one student is number 1, another is number 2, and so on to number 6. The reason for this limit is that it is not only an easy way to group, but it's also an easy way to switch kids for different activities. For example, "All the 2s get together for the warm-up," or "The odd numbers are on a team, and the even numbers are on the other team." The following is an example of how a class of 30 could be set up:

Team A	Team B	Team C	Team D	Team E
1	1	1	1	1
2	2	2	2	2
3	3	3	3	3
4	4	4	4	4
5	5	5	5	5
6	6	6	6	6

Obviously, in this setup there would be five number 1s, five number 2s, and so on. This setup is a time-efficient way to organize activities throughout the year.

To add some creativity to this format, students could create team names instead of numbers. For example, students could model their teams after five professional football teams.

Team 1	Team 2	Team 3	Team 4	Team 5
Bronco	Bronco	Bronco	Bronco	Bronco
Viking	Viking	Viking	Viking	Viking
Ram	Ram	Ram	Ram	Ram
Packer	Packer	Packer	Packer	Packer
Falcon	Falcon	Falcon	Falcon	Falcon

In this format, each team would have a Bronco, Viking, Ram, Packer, and Falcon. When teachers want to switch teams for a special activity, they could say, "All the Broncos together today."

Another way to make team designations fun is to do it by assigning each student in the team a sport. For example, each team could have a soccer player, runner, swimmer, golfer, basketball player, tennis player, and so on. When teachers want to organize a large group into two teams, they could simply say, "Golfers, swimmers, and basketball players on one team; runners, tennis players, and soccer players on the other team."

Motivators

Most physical educators are probably not too concerned with how their students are feeling emotionally as they walk in the door. In fact, physical education often goes with the attitude "the tougher, the better." With what we now know about learning, motivation, and how they are both directly related with emotion, such an attitude needs to change. The students need to recognize each other in a friendly and respectful way, and the teachers must make sure it happens. The most obvious way would be for teachers to model the behavior themselves. According to Rogers, Ludington, and Graham (1998), "When we develop one-on-one relationship skills—becoming aware of and tending to the emotional needs of students—we enter the realm of learning as well. If learning in school meets students' emotional needs, they will more likely engage in learning. School becomes a more motivating place to be."

To establish that sense of belonging and that feeling of significance, we need to make sure that all children know and feel that it truly does matter that they came. This feeling needs to be established immediately to make them feel more comfortable and to help eliminate any fears they may have walking into class.

The motivator is the first component of the ritual, and it should be done each class period. We define *motivators* as enthusiastic verbal and physical actions in which each student gets recognized upon entering the gym. The motivator is either done immediately upon entering the gym or done in their individual teams. The purpose is to make students feel welcomed and to get them fired up for class! Another reason for the motivator is for students to not only learn how to acknowledge people in a friendly way but to understand the purpose of why it's important. So often as a teacher, I would see students in the hallway, and they would not say hello unless I said it first. Moreover, I would rarely see students (who are already sitting in class) acknowledge their classmates as they entered the classroom. They would look up at the person, make eye contact, then look away. This really sets an unfriendly tone, and it also makes it possible for some students to go through the whole day without being acknowledged. We need to make students aware of how greeting people can make them feel.

For example, in preparation for introducing motivators, ask your students how they would feel if they entered a room and everyone looked up at them . . . and then looked away. Afterward, change the scenario so that it ends with someone acknowledging them in a friendly way. Get them to realize how they make people feel with their actions. Are they the students who would do the look-away, or are they the ones that would smile, make eye contact, and say hello?

The following is the introduction out of Roxann Kriete's book *The Morning Meeting Book* (1999):

"It Mattered That I Came"

In the spring of my first year as a secondary school teacher, I got a letter from a student for whom I had a particular fondness, letting me know that she was dropping out of school. School wasn't making much sense to her and little that she was being asked to learn held much interest for her. She wrote, almost apologetically, that school just wasn't a place she felt she belonged. More than twenty years later, her words still seem profoundly sad to me: I will always remember how you said "Hi, Sue" as I walked into eighth period. It made me feel like it really mattered that I came.

It touched and pained me that something which seemed so small to me, an act I hadn't even been aware of, had meant so much to her. I vowed to learn something from it and became more intentional about greeting my students. I stationed myself by the door and tried to say a little something to each one as they entered, or at least to make eye contact and smile at every student, not just the ones like Sue for whom I had an instinctive affinity.

Gradually I realized how much I was learning at my post by the door. I observed who bounced in with head up and smile wide, whose eyes were red-rimmed from tears shed in the girls' room at lunch, who mumbled a response into his collar and averted his eyes every day for an entire semester. I didn't know what to do about much of it, but at least I was learning how to notice.

I have learned a lot since then. It is good for students to be noticed, to be seen by their teacher. But it is only a start, not enough by itself. They must notice and be noticed by each other as well.

Motivators can be done in a variety of ways, including the teacher just standing at the door as students enter and high-fiving them while saying their name. As easy as it may sound, it actually may be difficult because of back-to-back classes and the lack of time for setup and takedown before and after each class. The motivator, however, really shouldn't take more than two minutes. To ensure each student is enthusiastically recognized upon entering class, we now provide you with a number of motivators that we hope you can incorporate into your routine.

Examples of Motivators

• **Teacher-led motivator.** The teacher stands at the door and high-fives students as they walk in (figure 2.1). It's important that the teacher portray an enthusiastic attitude while saying hello and addressing each student by name. Enthusiasm is crucial. You want the students motivated for class, and you want them to know you're excited they're here!

• **Student-led motivator.** A predetermined student stands at the door and does the same as the previous example demonstrates. It's important that the student be a genuine volunteer, rather than be "appointed" by the teacher unwillingly. Before students take on this role, it's important to go over the attitude of the motivator. The teacher may want to model enthusiastic greetings with the students, then have them practice these greetings with each other (the teacher in this case, once again, being proactive). As a class, students could also brainstorm different greetings so that it doesn't

Figure 2.1   Giving students a high-five greeting portrays your enthusiasm.

always sound so redundant. For example, "Hello, Jim!" "Good to see you, Kathy!" "Welcome to class, Mark!" The student's responsibility is to greet each student by saying their name after the word or words chosen during the brainstorm. It needs to be stressed that the student motivator is an important role in making people feel welcomed and motivated. Before students are allowed to do it, this role should be practiced with one another. Teachers also need to stress that students cannot practice selective enthusiasm; that is, they can't be enthusiastic when they greet some and not when they greet others. This practice would totally defeat the purpose of the greeting, and students' feelings could end up being hurt. These issues need to be addressed and revisited throughout the year. More examples of how to get students to understand the meaning and importance of enthusiasm are listed on page 30.

• **Team handshakes.** Each team uses the team handshake they came up with at the beginning of the year. Each student is responsible for shaking each team member's hand while greeting and saying each one's name.

• **Other teams' handshakes.** Each team models their team handshake, and the rest of the class gets to use it to greet three other people. For example, "Today, we are going to greet each other using Team A's handshake. Team A, show us your handshake, and greet your teammates in your most enthusiastic way, making sure to say the name of the student you greet." Team A models their handshake as the rest of the class watches. "Now greet at least three other people using Team A's handshake." If five teams are in the class, then the class could then obviously use five different handshakes as motivators.

- **Like-number or athlete greetings.** Remember how each person on a team has a number or a name? For this motivator, all the runners would greet each other, as would all the swimmers, and so on. Students could use a simple high-five, or perhaps individual students could get more involved in the decision making. A student who has a birthday that month or a student who is a great encourager can pick the handshake that the class could use.

- **Team greetings.** One team stands at the door, high-fiving students as they run in. This is a fun motivator that is more like a cheer. This motivator is similar to when starters get introduced before a basketball game: Their teammates line up, and as the players' names get read, they run to center court, high-fiving their teammates on the way out. In this particular motivator, a team would stand in a line at the door, high-fiving the rest of the class as they run in. Instead of "Hello, Jim" or "Welcome, Mark," it would be more like a cheer. For example, students could say, "Way to go, Jim!" "You're awesome, Mark!" "All right, Tina!" Again, students could brainstorm possible ways to cheer on their teammates in this motivator. Hopefully, they get loud and crazy in this one because ultimately we want them to be fired up! Once students have the opportunity to lead the motivator, this one would be the ideal to start with. Students are a lot more comfortable motivating others when they are with their team, rather than by themselves. Expect them to be a bit quiet the first time their teams do this motivator, but don't worry—the more they get to know and trust those around them, the more enthusiastic they become.

- **Two-team greetings.** This one can get really loud and crazy! But what a fun experience for someone who will never have the opportunity to be on a team outside of school. This motivator is similar to the previous one, but in this case, two teams stand at the door, one team at each side. As students enter, they greet and high-five classmates on both sides. Again, the teams doing this motivator should be encouraged to really get into it and enthusiastically cheer their teammates as they enter the gym.

- **Like-number greetings at the door.** Instead of having like numbers greet each other (1s greet the 1s; 2s greet the 2s . . .), have like numbers stand at the door to greet the rest of the class. Or, when names and sports are used within each team, you can say, for example, "The runners are in charge of the motivator next class period," or "The Broncos will be high-fiving their classmates tomorrow." Remember to switch the teams standing at the door. In this situation, the teacher needs to let the students know their assignment ahead of time so that all the runners or all the Broncos know to get to class early to greet and motivate their classmates.

Weekly Sample Schedule of Motivators

The following is an example of a weekly schedule of motivators. We encourage you and your students to use your creativity to come up with more.

Monday: Teacher-led.

Tuesday: Individual teams do their handshake while saying each other's names.

Wednesday: A team stands at the door, high-fiving and cheering as the class walks or runs in.

Thursday: Team-led. One team models their handshake, and the rest of the class follows that example, greeting at least three other people.

Friday: Student-led. One or two students stand at the door greeting and high-fiving their classmates as they enter class.

Motivating With Enthusiasm

Enthusiasm adds fun and excitement to whatever we do. We know that teacher enthusiasm is an important factor in motivating students, but how can we get students to portray enthusiastic attitudes? First of all, it has to come from the students themselves; a teacher can't make a student be enthusiastic. The teacher has to model it as much as possible and hope that students will learn from example. Second, it's more likely that enthusiastic attitudes surface when students are excited about the class. The teacher must make physical education a place where all students want to be; therefore, enthusiasm can come naturally from its own participants. Last, the students could construct meaning for the words *enthusiasm* and *motivation* with their teammates. Maybe some students could model enthusiasm, and the rest of the class could state the characteristics that displayed enthusiasm. Ask the students, "What does enthusiasm sound like? Look like? Feel like?" Get them to draw upon their own experiences of how they feel when they are around someone who is enthusiastic.

Some students are always a bit more enthusiastic than the rest. Hopefully, these students volunteer to be the motivators at the door early on in the year. If some students never volunteer to be at the door, that is fine. Maybe some of the more reserved students will be more enticed to take on that role if they have the option of having a partner to stand and greet with.

A Friendly Approach to Teaching

In her article "Enthusiasm and Feedback: A Winning Combination" (2001), Monica Parson, from Elon College in North Carolina, gives teachers specific tactics they can use to appeal to students on a positive emotional level. For example, she recommends that you try the following in your classroom.

1. Vary the way you speak; alter your pitch, tone, and volume. Show some excited speech if you want to fire up your students.
2. Look students directly in the eyes when you talk to them. This conveys to them that you have an interest in what they are doing. Widen your eyes and raise your eyebrows to show excitement in their accomplishments.
3. Use facial expressions to show your excitement about what it is you are presenting in your lesson. Remember one of the golden rules growing up—smile.
4. Express your emotions and your feelings. Show your happiness or your disappointment.
5. Encourage your students. All of your students need encouragement to be able to do their best. Encouragement is a way to instill confidence in your students. Give encouraging feedback such as "good job," "way to go," or "you can do it" to tell students exactly what is good. It gives them genuine motivation to improve.

So, to all you drill sergeants out there—try being genuine. Show a genuine interest in the students; use your sense of humor; and above all, demonstrate a little enthusiasm!

Choosing the Motivator

Having a set schedule for motivators is ideal. Students can come to class and do them on their own without teacher instruction. For example, if teams

000

are on a rotating schedule, then each team knows ahead of time when it is their turn. For example, if every Wednesday is team-motivator day and if the teams go in alphabetical order, then each team should (in theory) know when it's their turn. To help remind one another, however, the team that motivates at the door one week could remind the team who will be motivating the next week. Say, for example, a student is motivating at the door every Friday. After that student is done, the teacher and class may thank him or her. Then, the next student could immediately be assigned for the following Friday. While this is an optimal situation, it may take awhile to get there.

Once the students get used to a schedule, the teacher should wean them from the instructions to encourage them to get going on their own. At this point, the instructions should turn to questions. For example, "What team is leading the handshake today?" "Could you please show us what to do?" "What do you need to remember when greeting a classmate?" When the teacher doesn't have a set schedule, the motivator could be assigned the prior class period. For example, "Who hasn't had a chance to be the motivator at the door and would like to be?" In this case, the student or students who volunteer know that they can either stand at the door and motivate students as they walk in, or they can simply have a handshake ready to model by saying, "Motivate everyone on your team with this handshake, and remember to say their name while greeting them."

The eventual goal, around the third or fourth month, is for students to take the initiative without any instruction by the teacher. The first couple weeks of class, the teacher may want to be responsible for the motivator so that it could be modeled in an enthusiastic way. The only other motivators we suggest those first couple of weeks are the ones that are done in individual teams—the reason being that it's very important to say each student's name, and students may not know everyone's name those first couple weeks. It helps when they get to know their teammates on a more intimate basis before they are responsible for knowing everyone in the class.

If no one volunteers to be at the door, the teacher could simply say, "Team B will be the motivators at the door next class period." Or, the teachers could take on the role themselves. It's unlikely, however, that no one will volunteer. If it does happen, it may be more likely to occur early in the year when students don't feel comfortable with each other. When the right atmosphere is created and when students feel safe being fired up and enthusiastic around each other, they will want to take on the role of "Motivator at the Door."

Be aware that the same four or five students will continually be the ones to volunteer. There is nothing wrong with that, especially if they do a good job welcoming their classmates. The goal, however, is for as many students as possible to feel comfortable enough to take on that role. Be careful not to let the same students do it over and over without encouraging the others to take it on as well. If it seems as though the "Motivator at the Door" is unpopular among students, don't try to cover up the issue or push it on them. Be honest about it and ask them. Make it the subject of a huddle activity (which is discussed later in this chapter). Whatever you do, don't get mad at them. There is obviously an underlying issue here. So often when there are conflicts in the classroom, whether it is misbehavior or lack of motivation, we as teachers blame the students: "This group of kids just doesn't get it." "I'm not going to get anywhere with them." "They have no idea what respect means." Instead of taking on these kinds of attitudes, we need to focus on the underlying problem. Be honest and upfront about problems; trying to resolve them is a good lesson for the students, anyway. What do we want our students to do when they come across a problem in their lives? Do we want them to bury it and ignore it, or do we want them to be forthright with it and talk about it? By resolving problems both in the class and with the class, the teacher is modeling valuable life skills.

Forming Connections Through Huddles

The next component after the motivator is the team *huddle*. The purpose of the huddle activity is for students to relate their own lives and experiences to physical education and to use those experiences to build character and strengthen relationships. Students always participate in their huddle activities within their teams, and most huddle activities consist of character-building discussion activities. Because of time constraints, this component is the only one that is not done on a daily basis. However, as mentioned earlier, students still always meet with their team first, whether they have a huddle activity or not.

Facilitating Successful Huddle Activities— It's a Continual Process

We feel it is the teacher's responsibility to facilitate huddle activities the first month of school. However, by the second month, students should be encouraged to facilitate discussion within their teams to promote a sense of ownership and a feeling of empowerment. To make these discussions as meaningful as possible, the teacher must properly model and practice them. The teacher cannot simply hand each team a team talk the first day of school and expect the students to productively discuss it. More than likely, the students will be apprehensive and accomplish very little. The teacher needs to first discuss the responsibilities of being on a team. In fact, this discussion should take place with the whole group before students are actually assigned to teams.

First Week of Class

Students should not be placed on teams until the second week of school. During the first week of school, the students need to learn what makes a student a good team member. This can be done through the teacher's questioning, which can get the students to think about their own situations and what kinds of team members they are. The following are some sample questions.

- What are the characteristics that make a good team member?
- What does listening have to do with being a good team member?
- Think of some teams you have been on in the past. Were there people whom you didn't enjoy being on a team with? What were some of their characteristics? How about the people whom you did enjoy being on a team with? What were their characteristics?
- In your fitness journal, write down what kind of teammate you think you are. What are some of your positive characteristics? What are some areas you need to work on? Remember, this does not have anything to do with your athletic skills; it only has to do with what kind of teammate you are. (For this last set of questions, assure the students that they don't have to share their answers with the whole group, but remind them that they are questions they should be definitely thinking about.)

After the teacher asks each question, the students should have a chance to write down their responses, making sure they are really giving thought to the question. As students share their answers to the first three questions, the teacher could write down their responses on a piece of paper, which could then be hung in the gym. Students should place this piece of paper in their portfolio, and it could be considered their baseline for themselves as a teammate (baselines and portfolios are explained in chapter 4). After giving them time to write, ask the students to share their responses with the group, and encourage discussion on each topic. If you don't want to take up the whole class period on this topic, students could write down their responses during the first class meeting, then discuss them during the next class meeting. This way, students can participate in some physical activities that day as well.

Second Week of Class

Teachers should assign teams only when they feel as though the students have a firm grasp on what it means to be a good teammate. To assess whether the students comprehended the meaning of being a good teammate, teachers could check for understanding by observing students in a group activity that first week of school, in addition to reading their responses to the previous questions. For instance, the teacher could say, "Now we are going to play a game. I want to see if you can put your words into actions. You stated that not putting down your teammates or the other team was important. You also stated that you were going to involve everyone on your team. Now you need to show me what you mean by modeling the behaviors you described."

When the game is over, the class could quickly state the behaviors they witnessed that supported what they discussed last week. Hopefully, teachers can determine the teams by the second week of school. They also need to explain to the students that once their teams are established, they will always report to their teams upon entering the gym.

First Huddle Activity—Learning How to Praise and Encourage

In the first huddle activity, students should learn how to praise and encourage. At a conference on facilitating responsibility through physical activity, Debbie Vigil, winner of the 1994 NASPE (National Association of Sports and Physical Education) Elementary Physical Education Teacher of the Year, demonstrated a great technique to teach praise and encouragement. With it, she reinforced our belief that you cannot just tell students to praise and encourage one another. You must teach them what praise and encouragement actually are, then give them practice situations to use their new skills. Perhaps starting the year with this lesson would be an effective introductory technique to get children to understand what kind of place this gym environment is. With your large group, pose the following question: "What is praise, and when would you use it?" On a large chart, write the heading *Praise* in big letters, and beneath it, write two subheadings, *Hear* and *See* (figure 2.2).

Ask the students to give examples of praise that you can hear, and list these under the *Hear* column. Follow this by asking students to give examples of praise you can see. List their responses under the *See* column. Duplicate this process by using an encouragement chart (figure 2.3).

When your students finish giving examples of encouragement that they can hear or see, give them the opportunity to practice using these terms in a physical activity, such as the following.

Praise	
See	**Hear**

Figure 2.2 Praise chart.

Encouragement	
See	**Hear**

Figure 2.3 Encouragement chart.

Praise and Encouragement Practice

Each group practices the rope-jumping skill called the Egg Beater (figure 2.4).

Four students turn the ropes, one student is the jumper, and the sixth student is the recorder. Provide a worksheet, pencil, and clipboard for the recorder. The turners and jumper rotate positions so that all the turners get a chance to jump. The recorder does not have to rotate. Students can add the advanced skill of jumping a short rope inside the egg beater as well.

While both the turners and jumpers practice their skills, just the turners practice their praise and encouragement skills. The recorder then records the responses of the jumping team on a social skills observation sheet (figure 2.5).

After the students have had time to practice the physical skill of jumping rope, bring them back into a large group for discussion. The recorders can now give the class their information on their observations. Reporting to the large group not only gives students recognition for their social skills, but it also allows the class to evaluate what has occurred. Additionally, you may pose some questions to the class at this time.

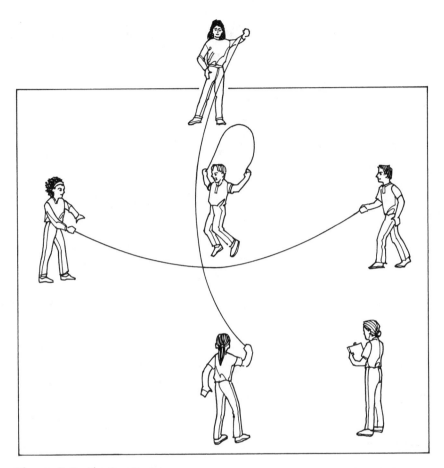

Figure 2.4 The Egg Beater.

- Were any put-downs or criticisms used?
- How do put-downs make you feel?
- How did being praised make you feel?
- How were you encouraged?
- Is it hard to praise or encourage another person?
- Was it hard to receive the praise or encouragement?

Ms. Vigil's lesson is one way to use praise and encouragement in an activity lesson. These social skills need to be practiced and reinforced just as we practice and reinforce physical skills.

Social Skills Observation Sheet		
Name	**See**	**Hear**

Figure 2.5 Social skills observation sheet.

Second Huddle Activity—Constructing a Team Pact

The second huddle activity is for teams to make a plan on how they are going to be a successful team. This activity could be done about the third week of school. From these guidelines, the teacher could highlight consistencies among teams and post them as "Our Class SOP" (standard operation procedures).

The teacher may say, "Your team needs to come up with guidelines to ensure success. What needs to happen with each teammate for your team to function as positively and productively as possible? Think about what we have talked about the last couple weeks. What did you learn about the characteristics of a good team member? With these questions in mind, go ahead and determine your guidelines. These guidelines are going to be called your 'team pact.' Once you have finalized your team pact and everyone agrees on it, each team member needs to sign it. Determine a fair way to designate who will be the recorder for your team." Each team could then be responsible for coming up with eight guidelines (see figure 2.6).

Figure 2.6 Students work together to form a team pact.

The following is an example of what a fifth-grade team may come up with while determining their team pact.

Team Pact

for _____

Team name

For our team to be successful, all members will adhere to the following guidelines: (Be specific, if you say everyone needs to respect each other, what does that mean? What behaviors show respect?)

- No put-downs.
- Encourage teammates when they make a mistake, when they are down about something, and when they are doing something that is really hard.
- Praise teammates when they do something good.
- Listen to whoever is talking and don't interrupt.
- Don't always just sit by friends in huddle activities.

- Include everyone on the team and be nice to them.
- Always high-five each other after class.
- Don't always be the one that has to go first.
- Find a fair way to make decisions.
- Help teammates solve problems.

Third Huddle Activity—Determining Team Name, Team Handshake, and Cheer

After teams have come up with their team pact, they should have an opportunity to share it with the rest of the class. During the first month or two, team pacts should be displayed whenever there is a huddle activity. They can be either permanently hung on the wall or simply given to the teams before they participate in a huddle activity. Before they participate in the activity, however, teams should together read over their pact to remind themselves of what they decided and to ensure continued success as they participate in activities as a team. After the first few months, the pacts should only be revisited as often as the teacher sees fit—maybe every other month, or whenever the teams need a gentle reminder.

Now that the teams have determined their pacts, their next huddle activities are to determine their team names, handshakes, and cheers. We have this as the third activity because there is potential conflict in determining a team identity. This is essentially a team-building activity, and by having their pact in place, they are more prepared to work through conflicts in a constructive way—more so than they would if this were the first or second huddle activity.

Time Concerns

It may seem as though these initial huddle activities will take up a lot of class time the first few weeks. We encourage you to keep our vision in mind of what we are trying to accomplish, a love for fitness that lasts a lifetime. We believe that by being proactive and letting the students construct guidelines for their team (and, ultimately, the class), the benefits are overwhelmingly positive and time is thus saved in the long run. In addition, time spent on these team activities also creates a feeling of belonging that many students desperately need. By laying this important groundwork, you are well on your way to creating a responsive physical education classroom.

After your classes have completed these initial activities, we recommend doing a huddle activity once every one or two weeks in the form of the discussion prompts, which we provide in the upcoming sections. The individual teacher needs to determine when and how often to use huddle activities based on the needs of the class.

Team Huddle Captains

Each team should have a captain, as designated by the teacher, that changes weekly or every other week. We recommend the teacher choose the natural leaders at first and from there use a rotating schedule to ensure that everyone gets a turn. The captains' responsibilities range from their reading team talks to facilitating conflict resolution among teammates to even being responsible for reporting any absences to the teacher. Allow students to develop a list of behavioral characteristics that the captain should display. Captains take on a leadership role, so it's important that they understand what exactly that means. This subject would also be great for a huddle activity. A good outside assignment for the captains would be for them to write or find their own team talk and share it with their team. Of course, this assignment would be only after the students have seen several examples of team talks.

Huddle Activity Discussion Prompts

In the following sections, we provide more than 50 discussion prompts for students to use during huddle activities. These activities are written prompts that can be in the form of real-life situations, where students apply prior knowledge for better understanding, or they can be in the form of an inspirational saying, which encourages kids to think more abstractly to make meaning. Whatever the format may be, students process the meaning by giving specific examples of how it relates to their lives. The prompts should initially be facilitated by the teacher, but as the year goes on, we hope students (via their captains) can facilitate them within their teams as well. In addition, it would be great if students could start providing their own discussion prompts. They could write about their own experiences and include discussion questions, or they could bring in their favorite quotes or readings. Discussion prompts come in four formats: focus words, inspirational sayings, reflection scenarios, and stories.

Focus Words

As teachers, we need to take time to teach and highlight certain values that we want our students to exhibit in physical education. One avenue we can take to accomplish this objective is through the use of discussion prompts. The first example of discussion prompts to be used during huddle activities is *focus words*, and we suggest a list of 20. The purpose of the focus words is to bring meaning to words that are essential in developing good character.

These words should be highlighted in the gym, and the meaning of these words should be constructed by the students, with a meaningful discussion to follow. Of course, physical education is an activity class; long discussions simply cannot happen every class period. However, if the teacher could introduce and discuss with the class one word every two weeks, it would go a long way to promote ethical behavior. If teachers do not feel that they can take the time for discussion, then perhaps the word and meaning can be introduced in class with the discussion questions being sent home for the parents to administer. Another option would be to carry it over into the regular education classroom. (We're always looking for ways to connect disciplines, and this would be a great opportunity.) Wouldn't it be powerful to fill the gym walls with posters made by the students with their meanings and examples of these words? They would feel empowered, as well as a sense of ownership, seeing their work on the walls.

Focus Word: Respect

Definition: A feeling of honor or esteem for something or someone

Story line: During competition, show respect for your opponents, your teammates, and the officials. If you understand that everyone is doing their best, then show them respect for their efforts.

Discussion questions:

- What does respect mean to you?
- Do you want people to respect you?
- What are some ways you can earn respect?
- What makes you respect others?
- Have you ever seen anyone show disrespect for any fellow teammates?
- For their opponents?
- For the officials?
- What did you think of that behavior?
- Can you respect property as well as a person?

Knowledge never hurt anyone. We can't assume our students know the meaning of these words. Allowing them to construct a definition and make meaning of the word is an effective way to put a priority on the importance of the behavior the team represents.

Bringing a high school athlete into your classroom once a week to lead the discussion would add volume to its importance.

Let's look at other words and see how we can direct the discussion of the word into a context of physical education and competition.

Focus Word: Honesty

Definition: Truthful and trustworthy, not lying, stealing, or cheating

Story line: George Washington, our first president, said the best title a person can possess is that of being honest.

Discussion questions:

- What does honesty mean to you?
- Can you think of anyone you know who is completely honest?
- Can someone be dishonest during a game? How?
- What would happen if teams with dishonest players competed against one another?
- Is taking performance-enhancing drugs dishonest? How?

Focus Word: Sportspersonship

Definition: One who observes the rules of a contest and accepts victory or defeat without behaving boastfully or angrily

Story line: We should all play hard, but we should play fair and be honest with our teammates and opponents. Try to be the best you can be, but be considerate and fair in the treatment of others.

Discussion questions:

- What does being a good sport mean to you?
- How can someone be a good sport?
- Why do you think being a good sport is important?
- Have you ever been a poor sport? What did you do to become a poor sport at that time?
- Can parents be poor sports? How?
- Can coaches be poor sports? How?

Focus Word: Trust

Definition: To have confidence or firm belief in the honesty or dependability of someone or something

Story line: You have to trust in your future: If you prepare and work hard, your dreams will come true.

Discussion questions:

- What does trust mean to you?
- Are there certain people you trust more than others? Why?
- What makes people trustworthy?
- How can you show trust in your coach or teacher?

Focus Word: Judgment

Definition: A decision reached after careful consideration of evidence; the ability to choose wisely

Story line: You are the best judge of what you can do and what you cannot do; be honest with yourself and do what is right.

Discussion questions:

- What does judgment mean to you?
- What are some judgments you need to make during the school day?
- Do some judgments include thinking about the effect your decision has on other people?
- Make up a situation that would require you to use good judgment, then act out the situation. Try it again—only this time, act out the situation using bad judgment. Example: During physical education class, your team is playing basketball against your best friend's team. Your team loses a close game, and your friend taunts you. Your friend is only kidding, but you get very angry. What do you do?

Focus Word: Pride

Definition: A sense of one's dignity or worth

Story line: Always do your best in school and life. Give your best effort. If you do not, you cheat yourself and others. Take pride in yourself.

Discussion questions:

- What does pride mean to you?
- How do you cheat yourself if you do not do your best?
- How can athletes take pride in their sport?
- How can students take pride in their school work?
- Can you take pride in your behavior and treatment of others?
- How many have pride in their school? Why or why not?

Pride

Definition: A sense of one's own dignity or worth.

GOPHER

Focus Word: Integrity

Definition: Strict personal honesty and independence

Story line: You must believe in your own honesty and character before you can believe in anyone else's. People believe in you when you have integrity.

Discussion questions:

- What does integrity mean to you?

- Integrity has another meaning. It can also mean *unity* or *completeness*. What does the following statement mean to you: "The integrity of the team has been kept."

- I think the meaning of integrity is that you can be honest and fair even if no one else is behaving that way. That sounds hard. Do you think you could do it?

Focus Word: Character

Definition: A person's normal nature or behavior

Story line: Build your house on a strong foundation of brick and mortar so that it stands for 100 years. Build your character on a foundation of honesty, respect, and discipline so that your reputation stands for 100 years.

Discussion questions:

- What does character mean to you?

- Does your character include many behaviors, such as honesty, fair play (being a good sport), and respect?

- What is the difference between having character and being a character?

- What do you think is the best part of your character?

Focus Word: Poise

Definition: Dignity and possession (or control) of your behavior and composure

Story line: How you respond to events that involve you shows whether you have poise. Sometimes it is very hard to keep your poise or composure when you are angry or upset. If, however, you are a strong person, you can do it.

Discussion questions:

- What does poise mean to you?
- Have you ever seen people lose their poise?
- Think about what it would be like to lose your composure during a game.
- Do you think keeping your poise helps you concentrate?
- Can you think of another word that starts with *P* that means the opposite of poise? Answer: Panic

Focus Word: Class

Definition: Great style or quality

Story line: If you have class, people will recognize it. If you have class and are fortunate to win a game, you won't taunt, boast, or brag. If you have class and lose, you don't make excuses or blame others. That's class.

Discussion questions:

- What does class mean to you?
- What are some things you can do after winning a game that show class?
- What are some things you can do after losing a game that show class?
- Can you show class in the way you dress?
- How can you show class by the way you treat people?

Focus Word: Loyalty

Definition: Being faithful to a person, country, idea, or conduct

Story line: If you are part of team, school, community, or family, you should be faithful to them. Surround yourself with people you can count on and who can count on you.

Discussion questions:

- What does loyalty mean to you?
- What does it mean, "You can count on me"?
- What are some things you should be loyal to?
- How can you be loyal to your teammates?
- Can you be loyal to something or someone that you don't like or agree with?

Focus Word: Unselfishness

Definition: Being generous and thinking of others

Story line: Always try to make someone's day a little better. When playing a game, think about being a good teammate, and be unselfish with your encouragement.

Discussion questions:

- What does unselfishness mean to you?
- When you help someone else achieve, how does that make you feel?
- Give an example of something you can say to someone that would show you are an unselfish teammate.
- Does a team work better if no one is concerned about who gets the glory?
- If you get a lot of awards, it is due to your hard work. But remember—a lot of people supported you.

Focus Word: Caring

Definition: To be concerned about others; to look after others or take charge of their welfare

Story line: The world could use some more caring people. To be concerned about the feelings of others is a very noble act.

Discussion questions:

- What does caring mean to you?
- How can you show your teammates that you are a caring person?

Focus Word: Enthusiasm

Definition: Great interest and excitement about something

Story line: Find things about school and sports that excite you, then give 100 percent of your effort participating in them. You have to love what you are doing because it makes it so much easier to be enthusiastic about it.

Discussion questions:

- What does enthusiasm mean to you?
- Think about some things you are enthusiastic about.
- Do you find it hard to be enthusiastic about some things? Can you do anything to overcome that lack of enthusiasm? Perhaps by setting goals?
- Can you be too enthusiastic about something? What could happen?
- Find something to be enthusiastic about this week. See if enthusiasm spreads.

Focus Word: Students are responsible for this week's discussion

Definition:

Story line:

Discussion questions:

-
-
-

Focus Word: Courage

Definition: The quality of mind and spirit that helps one take risks and face hardship with confidence and control

Story line: There will be many things you will want to do in life, but sometimes you need a little courage to give it a try. You also need courage to develop a strong character.

Discussion questions:

- What does courage mean to you?
- Why does it take courage to develop a strong character?
- What does "courage of your convictions" mean?
- Does it take courage to be the best you can be in your favorite sport?
- Does it take courage to enter a race knowing it will be tough . . . but you enter it anyway?

Focus Word: Confidence

Definition: A good feeling about yourself and your abilities

Story line: Sometimes we are not so confident because we think we might fail. If you work hard and prepare, your confidence will grow. You won't be afraid of failure; you will look at it as just a temporary setback.

Discussion questions:

- What does confidence mean to you?
- Does having confidence mean you will be the best at something?
- How can you get more confidence?
- Can you have confidence in yourself and still lose or fail at something?
- Can you have confidence in your team? How can they have confidence in you?

- Do you have confidence in your everyday behavior?

Focus Word: Commitment

Definition: A pledge or obligation to follow a certain course of action

Story line: If you want to be as good as you can be at something, you have to be committed to it. Hard work and commitment help you reach your goals.

Discussion questions:

- What does commitment mean to you?
- Do you know how to set goals? Should they be written down, or should they be dreams in your head?
- How can teammates be committed to a team?
- How can you be committed to school?
- Take time tonight to write down one dream or goal. Think about how you can reach it.

Focus Word: Discipline

Definition: Controlled behavior formed by training or work that tends to mold a specific skill

Story line: When others fall behind or forget what's important, use your discipline to continue moving toward your goal.

Discussion questions:

- What does discipline mean to you?
- How is self-discipline different from the discipline your parents or teachers have for you?
- Do we all have self-discipline? What makes us want to use it?
- How do you discipline yourself to achieve a physical skill, such as shooting a basket?
- How do you discipline yourself to get good grades in school?
- If you discipline yourself, will others have to?

Focus Word: Principles

Definition: A statement or set of statements describing the way someone acts or behaves

Story line: Work hard in life, but also play hard—keep your life in balance. Wherever you end up, always remember your principles and how they help you accomplish your goals.

Discussion questions:
- What does principles mean to you?
- What are some beliefs we should have as to how people should act when playing a game?
- What would be one of the most important beliefs everyone should agree on when playing a game?

We have offered 20 words to teach and discuss. There are many more descriptive words you can come up with. Add to this list, watch your class' behavior, then decide which word they need to discuss. Let students decide on words to bring to class. The students can have a short discussion on the focus word in their huddle or while they walk the perimeter of the gym as a group.

Some people may argue that some of the words here do not belong in a character-education program. Surely, a caring person doesn't necessarily have to be enthusiastic to have good character. Maybe this list does contain words that are not all similar in nature, but they do describe behaviors that are good and behaviors that we definitely want to enhance in our students.

Inspirational Sayings

The next form of discussion prompts we propose is in the form of inspirational sayings. So often, we have posters and sayings up all over the gym or classroom, but we never really discuss their meanings or morals. Such opportunities to discuss an important lesson or value should not go unnoticed, as they are valuable lessons that need to be related to the students' lives. In the following sections, we provide over 20 inspirational sayings that students should discuss and find meaning from. This particular huddle activity doesn't need to take more than 5 or 10 minutes; it depends on how far the teacher wants to go. The first time students discuss an inspirational saying could be as a whole group (again, with the teacher modeling it first).

The saying could be up on a wall or handed to each student on a reproducible card as they walk in the door. The class could read it together, or a student may volunteer to read it out loud. Along with these sayings, teachers can ask three general questions to facilitate discussion.

- What does this saying mean?
- Give specific examples of how it relates to a situation in physical education or in your lives.
- Now that you understand this saying, how might it affect your actions or thoughts in the future?

After the teacher facilitates these discussions once or twice, the teams could then be responsible for taking over the discussion among themselves. Team captains could be given the saying on a sheet of paper. They could read it out loud and then ask the general questions listed above.

As opposed to store-bought posters, some teachers have students make up their own inspirational sayings and hang them on the walls. When Michelle Robinson, a teacher in Anoka, Minnesota, gave her class this task, a fifth-grade boy came up with "A great way to get in the last word is by saying you're sorry."

Inspirational Saying #1

Everyone is endowed with qualities of a champion and can succeed in spite of handicaps in the most important game of all—the game of life.

Alice Marble, Portrait of a Champion

Inspirational Saying #2

When we criticize another person it says nothing about that person, it merely says something about our own need to be critical.

Richard Carlson, Don't Sweat the Small Stuff

Inspirational Saying #3

Anger must be the energy that has not yet found its right channels.

Florida Scott Maxwell, "The Measure of My Days"—Reader's Digest

Inspirational Saying #4

Take chances, make mistakes. That's how you grow. Pain nourishes your courage. You have to fail in order to practice being brave.

Mary Tyler Moore, The Edge

Inspirational Saying #5

Reputation is what you're perceived to be. Character is what you really are.

John Wooden, Life's Playbook for Success

Inspirational Saying #6

Each team will make up a saying today.

Inspirational Saying #7

One of the most important things I've learned from sports is that you just don't win every time. And you're not supposed to. It sound mundane, but life is like that. You're not supposed to win every game.

Leroy Selomn, Life's Playbook for Success

Inspirational Saying #8

Everyone has responsibility to leave the world in a little better state than when he/she arrived. Can you leave your family, your room, your desk, your friends, this gym in a little better state than when you arrived? How?

Anderson and Glover

Inspirational Saying #9

Do you think when we play competitive games it is a bad thing? Why would it be bad? Should we quit playing competitive games, or should we change our attitudes?

Anderson and Glover

Inspirational Saying #10

Can we all set goals in various parts of our lives? Some of us already do. Make your goals hard to reach so that you are striving to attain them.

Anderson and Glover

Inspirational Saying #11

The object is not to see through one another, but to see one another through.

Peter DeVries, Because of You

Inspirational Saying #12

Here is the test to find whether or not your mission on earth is finished. If you're alive, . . . it isn't.

Richard Bach, Because of You

Inspirational Saying #13

A smile is the light in the window of your face that tells people that your heart is at home.

Unknown, Because Of You

Inspirational Saying #14

Things you do for other people are usually among the best things you do. Have you done something for someone today? It doesn't have to be a big thing, maybe just a smile and a friendly Hello!

To Your Success, Because of You

Inspirational Saying #15

Many people "talk" a good game, but actions speak louder than words. Don't just say you are going to help someone, expend the effort and do it.

Anderson and Glover

Inspirational Saying #16

If you are on a team, be loyal to your teammates and coach. Many times the team may not function smoothly, but complaining only makes it worse.

Anderson and Glover

Inspirational Saying #17

Coaches, teammates, and opponents can all make mistakes during a competitive game. There are, however, more people involved in this contest . . . "the officials." They may make mistakes also. How do you react when they make a decision you don't agree with?

Anderson and Glover

Inspirational Saying #18

Today's school students will be the leaders of tomorrow. To be a good leader, you must be honest, responsible, and willing to put the best interests of everyone before personal gain.

Sid Luckman, The Edge

Inspirational Saying #19

Any fool can criticize, condemn, and complain . . . and most fools do.

Dale Carnegie, The Edge

Inspirational Saying #20

In physical education class, we will be playing sports and games. You will win some games, and you will lose some games. Whatever the outcome, always do your best, play hard, and have fun. How you behave after the game will display your character.

Anderson and Glover

Inspirational Saying #21

When playing competitive games in physical education, be prepared to give others some glory. Be prepared to help and support your teammates.

Anderson and Glover

Inspirational Saying #22

Everyone is different in some way. Some have better ability in math or spelling. Some have faster running speed than others. Are you tolerant of those who do not have the same strengths as you?

Anderson and Glover

Reflection Scenarios

These particular discussion prompts are in the form of real-life situations that students can easily relate to. Students will understand these scenarios using prior knowledge and experience, and the situations are more than likely going to be ones they have already been in and will be in again. By constructing a way of handling these scenarios, students will be better prepared for the specific conflict and thus handle it in a positive way.

Being a Good Sport and Practicing Fair Play

A fourth-grade class was playing dodge ball for physical education one day. The blue team had won the first two games, and it was obvious the green team was beginning to get frustrated. They were starting to yell at each other for making mistakes. The class played a third game, and once again the green team lost. As the blue team celebrated, a member of the green team ran up to the teacher and said in an angry voice, "These teams aren't fair!" Another player from the same team yelled, "They cheated!"

- Were the players on the green team who were yelling at their teammates and complaining to the teacher helping their team in any way?
- How do those people look to the rest of the class?
- What could they have done to help their team?

- If your team just lost three games in a row, what could you do to show you are a good sport?

Theme: Poor sporting behavior

Team Behaviors

The Saints were playing for the regional championship. The winner of the game would advance to the state high school basketball tournament. The team that lost would be done for the year. It was a great game that came down to the final seconds. The Saints were down by one, with three seconds left when Mark, the Saints' point guard, got fouled while going up for a jump shot. The foul gave him two shots at the free throw line, which meant he could pull his team ahead by one if he made them both. The crowd was going wild as Mark calmly stepped up to the line. He missed the first one, but he still had a chance tie the game. The second shot rolled around the rim twice and bounced out. The Saints lost the game and were out for the season. Mark fell to the floor in disappointment. John, Mark's teammate, put his arm around Mark and did everything he could to help him feel better. Phil, another Saints player, walked by Mark and gave him a very angry look.

- How do you think Mark felt when he missed both free throws?
- How do you think Phil made Mark feel when he gave him a dirty look?
- What do you think John could say to Mark to make him feel better?
- Would you rather have Phil or John on your team? Why?
- Now think to yourself . . . who are you more like, Phil or John? (For this question, you don't have to share with you thoughts with your teammates.)

Themes: Negative body language, good vs. bad teammates, encouraging gestures, loyalty, caring, commitment

Humble vs. Cocky Behaviors

Your class just finished running the mile for physical education. Sarah and Jake were the first to finish. Sarah ran around yelling, "I won, I won, I came in first place!" As people finished, she quickly told them her time and that she was the first to finish. Jake, on the other hand, ran back and began cheering on his classmates without mentioning a word about finishing first.

- What are some words that would describe Sarah?

- How about Jake?
- Would you rather have Sarah or Jake on your team?
- Think to yourself . . . who are you more like, Sarah or Jake? (For this question, you can keep your thoughts to yourself; you don't have to share them with anyone.)

Themes: Encouragement, class, character, integrity

Self-Evaluation or Honesty

Jack was evaluating himself on how well he followed his Individual Fitness Plan (IFP). He worked very hard on his plan and even did better that he thought he would. Because of how hard he worked, he reached the goal he set earlier in the unit. When it came time to give himself a grade, he gave himself a B because he was afraid his teacher would think that he wasn't being truthful or that he was bragging.

- How do you feel about what Jack did?
- Should Jack worry about what other people think of him, especially when he is being truthful?
- What grade should Jack have given himself? Why?
- What's the most important quality to have when evaluating yourself? Why?

Theme: Honesty

Self-Evaluation or Honesty

Jeff just finished a project that he didn't work very hard on. He waited until the last minute to start it, and he had to rush to get it done the night before it was due. When he turned his project in, he had to evaluate how well he thought he did and how hard he thought he worked.

He really wanted to get an A in the class, and this project was part of the final grade. On his evaluation, he wrote that he worked very hard and that he thought he deserved an A. He knew this wasn't true, but he figured no one would really know.

- How do you feel about what Jeff did?
- What would be the right thing to do?
- When his teacher read his evaluation and looked through his project, what do you think she thought?
- What do you think the teacher should do or say if she knows Jeff isn't being truthful in his evaluation?

- What's the most important quality to have when evaluating yourself? Why?

Themes: Honesty, integrity

Peer Evaluation

Sam and Lily were good friends. They were also partners for a peer-evaluation activity. They were supposed to evaluate each other's portfolio and provide feedback. Sam's portfolio was in rough shape. He didn't have any baselines or goals, and there was no order to his work. It was tough for Lily to follow his progress throughout the unit. Lily was worried that Sam would be mad at her if she was honest about the quality of his portfolio.

- What should Lily do?
- What's the purpose of providing feedback to others?
- What kind of friend is Sam if he got mad at Lily for being honest about his portfolio?
- How would Lily be hurting Sam if she wasn't honest?
- If you are evaluating your friends and you feel they aren't doing the best they can do, how could you tell them?
- What is your responsibility when you are evaluating someone else's work or skills?

Themes: Teamwork, understanding, honesty

Life Lesson

A few years ago at the Seattle Special Olympics, nine contestants, all physically or mentally disabled, assembled at the starting line for the 100-yard dash. At the gun, they all started out, not exactly in a dash, but with a relish to run the race to the finish and win. All, that is, except one boy who stumbled on the asphalt, tumbled over a couple of times and began to cry. The other eight heard the boy cry. They slowed down and looked back. They all turned around and went back. Every one of them. One girl with Down's syndrome bent down and kissed him and said, "This will make it better." All nine linked arms and walked across the finish line together. Everyone in the stadium stood, and the cheering went on for several minutes. People who were there are still telling the story. Why? Because deep down we know this one thing. What matters in this life is more than winning for ourselves. What truly matters in this life is helping others win, even if it means slowing down and changing our course.

- How do you feel about this story?
- Do you agree with what the other children did after the boy fell down? Why or why not?

Themes: Caring, compassion, loyalty

Always Picked Last

Stacy didn't like gym class. Sometimes she even woke up with a stomach-ache on days of gym because her classmates teased her. She realizes she isn't the most athletic person but she always tries her best. That doesn't matter to some other students, though, because no matter how hard she works, they still laugh and make fun of her.

One day when it was time to pick teams, the teacher appointed two captains to do it. Stacy dreaded this process because it always ended the same way. Again, she was picked last and the team she had to be on rolled their eyes and snickered as she walked over. Once again, she fought back tears and wanted to crawl in a corner and hide.

- Everyone has certain talents or strengths. Stacy happened to be very talented in music. Does she deserve to be treated the way her classmates treated her just because sports wasn't one of her strengths?
- How do you feel about the people who teased Stacy?
- What could her team or even a teammate have done to make Stacy feel better?
- If you know someone on your team or in your class who is not comfortable with an activity, instead of making them feel worse by putting them down, what could you do to make the situation better for them?
- What's a fair way to pick teams that won't hurt people's feelings?

Themes: Tolerance, respect, being a good sport, caring

No One Will Shake My Hand

Everyday in physical education, the students greet each other with a handshake or high-five. Some students in class, however, avoid certain classmates because they don't want to shake their hand. Jeff, especially gets avoided a lot and feels very sad during this activity. Jesse and Dennis recognize how the other classmates treat Jeff so they always make a point to go give him a high-five.

- How would you feel if some of your classmates didn't want to shake your hand?

- What is the purpose of greeting classmates and giving them a high-five or shaking their hand?
- How do you feel about the students who only greet or shake the hands of their special friends and avoid the rest of the class?
- How do you feel about Jesse and Dennis?
- What could we do as a class or a team if we see people hurting other peoples feelings?

Themes: Caring, tolerance, respect, integrity, loyalty, unselfishness, courage

Oops! I Forgot My Shoes Again

Katie, Molly, and Melissa always forget to bring proper attire for gym class. As a result, they are asked to sit out for the day's activities. This seems to be a small victory for the girls. When they do remember to bring the proper clothing, they simply stand in the gym or field watching all the action around them. They often make mean comments to each other about the other girls who are participating in the activity. The other girls are putting in their best effort and the comments upset them.

- Why do you think these girls make mean comments about their classmates?
- What could the teacher or the class do to help prevent this from happening?
- How would you feel if you were on a team with these three girls?
- Why do you think they keep forgetting their clothing and avoid participating in class?

Themes: Judgment, disrespect, not being a good sport, class

Feeling Left Out

Alan is new at school and doesn't have many friends. He and his mom have moved four times already this year and he's attended four different schools. By the time he starts meeting people, they have to move again. He's beginning to hate school because it's so hard always being new and not having any friends. He spends most of his time working by himself or sitting alone during free time. When it's time for gym or recess he tries to find a way to try to avoid them. He often tells the teacher he doesn't feel well or he wants to stay in and get his work done. He's embarrassed and uncomfortable and he wishes so badly that the other students would ask him to play with them.

- How would you feel having to always change schools and not know anyone?
- If you see a student feeling left out, what could you do to help them?
- Have you ever been told by other people that you can't play with them? How did that make you feel?

Themes: Acceptance, unselfishness, pride

Don't Make a Mistake if You're on My Team

Brenda was an excellent athlete and was very competitive. Her goal was to win no matter what. She often got very upset and yelled at her teammates who weren't as athletic as her. One day, while playing basketball, her best friend, Kim, tried to pass Brenda the ball and accidentally passed it to the wrong team. Brenda yelled at Kim for making the mistake and embarrassed her in front of the whole class.

- How do you think Kim felt when she made the mistake?
- Did Brenda help Kim or her team out by yelling at her?
- How do you think Kim felt after being yelled at?
- What can you do when your classmates make a mistake to help them feel better, not worse?

Themes: Tolerance, being a good sport, selfishness, disrespect, judgment

Good Athlete; Bad Teammate

Frank and Mark were two very good athletes. In fact, they were considered two of the best in the school. Mark was also a very good teammate; Frank was not. Mark never bragged about his skills, and he was always encouraging others. Frank, on the other hand, thought and acted as if he were better than everyone else. He frequently put down his teammates when they made a mistake, and he rarely said anything positive.

One day, the teacher allowed two students to pick teams. Mark was picked well before Frank. Frank couldn't figure out why he wasn't one of the first ones picked, considering he was such a good athlete.

- Why do you think Mark was picked first and Frank was picked later?
- Who would you rather have on your team?
- Do you like being on a team with those who think they are better than everyone else and who get mad at their teammates?

Themes: Being a good sport, judgment, class, loyalty

Storytelling

The final form of discussion prompts we suggest is by way of *storytelling*. Thomas Lickona's book *Educating for Character* (1991) is a very good resource for teachers, and we highly recommend it. In this book, Lickona suggests that storytelling is a powerful tool that helps in the moral education of kids. The sporting world provides us with many heroic stories about success, despite great handicaps or obstacles. If stories are a powerful moral tool, then physical educators should have a toolbox full. It shouldn't be too hard to find these stories and condense them for a quick, once-a-month story. The kids would love it. Here is an example of a story that teaches the values we are looking for.

Eric's Story

During my 10th year of teaching, I was asked to start an adapted physical education program in our district. Adaptive physical education is teaching sports, games, and other activities to children who have a disability. One of my very first students was a young man named Eric. Eric was a ninth grader when I met him. What I remember most of all is his great sense of humor. When we had class together, we worked hard on his fitness and skills, but we always ended the class with some jokes or funny stories. Everyone in school knew Eric and loved his sense of humor as much as I did.

In the fall of Eric's freshman year, I asked him what activity he would most like to learn. His answer: football. Well, I was concerned about Eric's ability to play football. He was very small, and he had a stroke when he was in the second grade. The stroke left Eric with extremely poor balance and a weak left side of his body. I tried to talk Eric out of football and into a sport that I would feel safer with. I felt a safer sport would be better for Eric's future enjoyment—something like bocce ball. Eric insisted upon football, so I taught him pass patterns. We practiced many different pass routes by diagramming them and putting out cones to mark the path. I threw him pass after pass with a small foam football. Eric rarely caught the ball, but he always rejoiced when he did and would raise his arms as if scoring a touchdown. My arm ached. We practiced pass patterns for about two weeks, then moved on to another activity. I could tell Eric was disappointed, but he was safe, I was comfortable, and he knew pass patterns.

In the fall of his sophomore year, Eric said, "Mr. Glover, I want to learn about football."

Eric was now in high school, and the football players were his heroes. He never missed a Friday night home game.

I said, "Well, okay, Eric. We will learn plays."

We practiced the dive, fullback, off-tackle, the sweep, the option, and the play-action pass.

"But, Mr. Glover, I want to play the game."

"Well, Eric, maybe next year we can get some friends from study hall and we can play. Meanwhile, let's learn some plays."

By learning plays and pass routes, I felt Eric would be a better, more knowledgeable spectator. So, we did not play the game during his sophomore year, and once again, both he and I got by another football season unscathed.

When Eric's junior year rolled around, I knew what was in store for me on the first day.

"Football, Mr. Glover. I don't want to learn any more plays or pass patterns. I want to play the game."

Well, Eric was a bit of a football expert by now, and I knew I couldn't keep from granting his wish sooner or later. I promised Eric that we would get some kids out of study hall in two weeks, and we would play the game. In the meantime, we had to practice our pass routes and plays so that we would be ready for the big game.

The Fateful Day Arrives

At the end of our two-week practice reviews, I met with Eric for class. It happened to be on a Friday, and with Eric waiting in the locker room, I went to study hall to get some kids to help us play a game of football. Imagine my surprise when I went to the study hall and found eight football players, all of whom had their jerseys on. They had a game that night, and it was common practice to wear the jersey on game day. I met with the guys and asked if they could help out for a half hour. They all knew Eric and readily agreed. I told them we will only have a few rules.

Walk, no running. (Eric could not run.)

No fooling around, be serious. Eric knows football, and he wanted them to treat him as a peer.

If I throw the ball to Eric, let him try to catch it. (Yes, I was the quarterback. I thought this would be the best way to protect Eric.) I told them I doubted he would catch it, but don't intercept or knock it down.

Can you imagine Eric's eyes when he saw me coming with eight football players!

We decided to play on the width of the soccer field, and we started our game close to the soccer goal. Our game proceeded, and I thought we were having a blast. The football players were great—they used all the correct terminology and there were a lot of high-fives and backslapping going on. I threw Eric a couple of passes, which he never caught, but at least he was having fun. About 20 minutes into the game, we had the ball right in front of the soccer goal, and we were marching toward our goal line. We were in the huddle, and as I was about to call a play, Eric said, "Mr. Glover, can I carry the ball?"

"Okay, Eric, let's run a sweep around left end. When I say 'blue,' you come in motion. After the ball is hiked, I will hand off to you and you run (walk) around the left end. Our left end and I will block for you."

Can you imagine this scene! It was a frosty fall day—we were playing on a hard, bumpy ground in front of the soccer goal. No grass, there was just dirt.

"Set!"

"Blue!"

Eric came in motion.

"Hut one!"

"Hut two!"

I spun and gave him the ball. Eric started his journey to the goal line. About halfway there, with the goal line only 10 yards away, Eric fell. His mind was going much faster than his feet could move. He fell hard; he landed on his face, right in the hard dirt. There was stunned silence. I thought, "Oh my gosh, I wanted him to have fun, but the last thing I wanted was for him to get hurt." We all gathered around Eric as I helped him up. His glasses were broken, and the fall put a gash on the bridge of his nose. His forehead was scraped, and the blood and the mud and the tears and the snot were all running down his face. He was a frightful sight. I had spent three years trying to protect him from physical pain, and now this happens. I cleaned him up as best I could and was about to dismiss class, but Eric wanted to finish the game. We had about eight minutes left in the class, so I agreed to finish. I asked Eric if he would like to watch from the sideline or finish by playing wide receiver. I figured that by playing wide receiver and never getting a pass thrown to him, he would be safe. He was still upset but chose to be wide receiver. With about four minutes left and five yards to go for a touchdown, we huddled for our final play. Before I could call the play, Eric spoke up. He was still gasping, as people who have been sobbing often do. He said—and I will never forget this—

"Mr. Glover, can I (sob) carry the (sob) ball again?"

I was stunned. I didn't know what to say. All of Eric's teammates were behind him and yelling, "Yeah, coach let him carry it again."

I was apprehensive but ultimately agreed.

"Set."

"Blue."

"Hut one."

"Hut two."

I spun, gave the ball to Eric, and he weaved his way through the masses of bodies that were trying to block for him and trying to stop him. He crossed the goal line, spiked the ball, and threw up his arms in triumph. He scored his touchdown. The football players mobbed him, giving him high-fives and a lot of praise. After three years of learning football, after three years of trying to convince me, a reluctant teacher, to let him play, he scored his touchdown. Needless to say, we were all inspired.

Discussion Questions

- Who had to take risks in this story? Answer: Both Eric and the teacher
- Do you think Eric would have wanted to carry the ball again without encouragement and praise from his teammates?
- Who showed the greatest confidence in this story? Answer: Eric
- Even though Eric was crying, do you think he earned the respect of the football players? How?
- How did the football players discipline themselves? Answer: They didn't run or intercept passes.
- Was Eric enthusiastic about football?

Many stories in the sports world convey emotion and learning. The kids may want to find a story and bring it in. Watching the Olympics will also give you many stories to videotape and bring to class. Stories are such powerful teachers. When you read the students a story, read it with conviction and feeling, and have some discussion questions ready to enhance the meaning of the story. We recommend using stories at least once a month.

Conflict Resolution

Maybe the class is having some conflicts that aren't the subject of a team talk we have provided. In that case, the teacher may have to write a team talk specific to the class' situation and follow it with discussion questions that allow the students to construct a solution to the problem. This activity is great for the captains to facilitate. Each team could then report their solutions to the rest of the class.

Council Meetings

Another way of determining what to discuss would be for the students to be able to voice particular problems or concerns they are facing in physical education. A lot of times, things happen out of the teacher's view. As teachers, we think we are on top of things, but we don't always know what goes on behind the scenes. Students should be encouraged to speak up. Once a month, you could have a council meeting. This occurs when teams meet and share any concerns or questions they have about class with the team captain. The team captains then meet together, representing their teams, with the teacher while the rest of the class participates in their warm-up or designated activity. One at a time, the team captains state their concerns, and the teacher writes them down. After all of the concerns have been shared, the teacher addresses them one by one.

It's important in using this format that the teacher doesn't solve the problems for the students. The captains should be asked, "What do you think we should do in this situation?" Students really feel empowered when they are given a voice in the classroom. Once all of the problems have been addressed and everyone agrees on the solutions, the team captains go back and share what was said with their teams. This could be done while the team cools down together so that the students are still moving while discussing.

Saint Mary's University in Winona, Minnesota, does this activity in the form of a site council meeting with their students in the master's of education program. The students genuinely feel as though what they have to say matters, and it makes them feel valued and respected. Many of the teachers who have graduated from the program go on to use the format of the site council meeting in their own classrooms.

Role-Playing

Another great way to solve conflict is by role-playing. Each team compiles a list of conflicts they have experienced in physical education, and from there, they choose one and determine how they could possibly avoid that situation or resolve it. Each team then role-plays the situation to the rest of the class, who could be asked the following questions after each team completes their skit:

- What was the conflict in this situation?
- Raise your hand if you've ever been in the same situation.
- How did they handle the conflict?
- Do you agree with how it was handled?

- Do you have any other ideas in how this conflict could be handled positively?

This is obviously a time-consuming activity and one the teacher may not want to take class time for. Once again, it would be great if these activities could be done in language arts class or homeroom, but that would only work if the teams are in those classes together. If such is not the case, as it probably wouldn't be in many middle schools or high schools, then it would be well worth class time in physical education to discuss these issues before they take place. As these conflicts arise throughout the year, the teacher could simply ask the students, "Now what did you decide you were going to do in this situation?" More than likely, it was a situation that they already discussed with their teammates and could thus figure out how to resolve it with little teacher interaction.

Sample Schedule for a Two-Week Huddle Activity

Monday: Introduce the focus word *respect* to the class. The meaning, however, should be constructed by the students before the teacher gives the actual dictionary definition. The teacher could introduce the word and read the discussion questions to the whole class. To encourage more involvement, the teacher may read the questions, and each team can then discuss them in their huddles. For even more involvement, the teacher could hand the questions to the team captains, who would facilitate the discussion in their huddles.

Tuesday (or the next class period): Give the team captains a reflection scenario to read to their teams and lead a discussion within their huddle. It's essential that the subject of the reflection scenario is *respect*.

The following week: Reflection time for the students is the last activity involving the focus word, and it is probably the most important aspect of developing a deeper understanding. It should be done toward the end of the two-week period, and teachers can do it in a number of ways. Students would have a chance to reflect on how they themselves or their classmates displayed characteristics of *respect* during that two-week period. The following are ways students could partake in this reflection.

- **Written reflection.** Students would individually answer open-ended questions on a sheet of paper and include it in their portfolio. These reflection questions could even be handed out at the end of a class and given as homework. The questions should be associated with the focus word or the theme students are concentrating on for the given amount of time. The following are examples of questions that the teacher could ask if the focus of discussion for a two-week period was *respect*.

- Give some specific examples of respectful behaviors that you observed in others during the last couple of weeks.
- What respectful behaviors have you shown toward any of your classmates recently?
- Have any of your classmates shown respect toward you this week? What did they do, and how did it make you feel?
- On a scale of one to five, one being the worst and five being the best, rate yourself on how well you respect everyone, including adults, peers, siblings, and younger children. Please explain why you gave yourself the score you did.
- How do you hope to improve in this area?

• **Pair share.** At the beginning of each year, quarter, or semester, the teacher would assign everyone a partner. (These could be their "fitness buddies," which are talked about in chapter 4.) Instead of writing down the answers to the previous questions, the students would discuss their answers with their partners. On the days of pair-share time, it would be a good idea for teachers to have the partners warm up or cool down together to maximize their time together. It's crucial that students use this time wisely and don't turn it into a gossip session about other students who didn't display respectful behaviors. These conversations should remain positive, focusing on themselves and not others. Teachers could ask their students before they participate in pair-share activities the following questions:

- What do you think is the purpose of discussing topics with a partner?
- What is your responsibility when your partner is talking?
- What can you do if your partner starts talking negatively about other students instead of focusing on her/himself? An important aspect in making pair-share time successful is establishing trust between the partners. Students aren't going to open up to each other if the trust isn't there.

• **Team reflection.** This could also be considered a huddle activity in which teams are given reflective questions to discuss. Again, the questions would revolve around the focus word. If a team reflection is going to take place, it would be good idea to have a light warm-up or cool-down of stretching so that they could be doing something together as they reflect. Teachers can call this a *moving and reflecting* session.

More examples of reflection questions are provided in chapter 4.

Strengthening Student Connections Through Warm-Ups

As mentioned in the introduction, the ritual at the beginning of class has three important components. We've already talked about the importance of motivators and huddles; now it's time to take a closer look at warm-ups. The purpose of the warm-up is to get the body physically warmed up for class and provide fitness experiences while having fun and strengthening the students' sense of community. These warm-ups are unique in that they are done in teams, rather than in traditional large groups. This puts the focus on developing team spirit and community. While some of the warm-ups presented here can be done in large groups, we feel each team should warm up together as much as possible, immediately following the huddle break. There may be some days, however, when the teacher could combine teams, and they could participate in the warm-up together. For example, "All the number 2s will participate in the warm-up together today," or "Odd teams are together today for the warm-up, and all even teams are together."

We now provide 27 sample team warm-ups for you to use. While warming up as an entire class should not be completely eliminated, we believe warming up in teams as often as possible will serve many purposes, including strengthening your students' team connections.

CIRCUITS
Grade Levels: 2-8

Equipment

- Circuit cards
- Jump ropes (6)
- Mats (2)
- Gym scooters (6)

Description and Setup

After the teammates have reported to their team huddle, the teacher should call each captain to come forward to get their team's circuit warm-up sheet. The teams must complete all activities on the sheet together, as a team. No one is allowed to run ahead and finish early. Each team has an identical set of circuit exercises, but they are in a different order. This prevents two teams from being at the same circuit at once. Consider playing some popular music while the students are warming up. We like using music as a signal: "Once the music starts, you may begin," or "When the music stops, please freeze." See figure 2.7 for a diagram of Circuits.

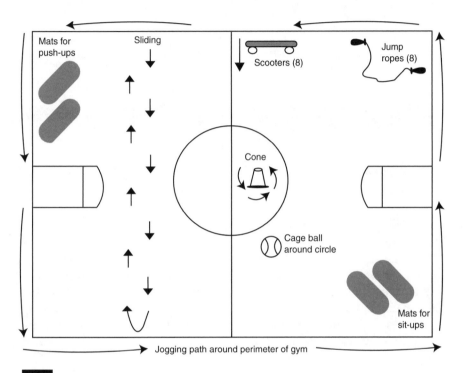

Figure 2.7 Gym setup for Circuits.

Sample Team Circuit Warm-Up

The following is for Team #1.

- Touch eight separate lines on the floor with your right hand.
- Complete 50 jump-rope repetitions.
- Jog five laps around the perimeter of the gym.
- Report to the push-up mat. Attempt 20 push-ups. You may use your knees if you get tired.
- Touch four separate walls with your left hand.
- Report to the sit-up mat. Attempt 20 sit-ups.

- Slide the width of the gym eight times.
- Report to the gym scooters. Lie on your tummy on the scooter. Scoot half the width of the basketball court six times, using your arms to propel the scooter.
- Sing a song with two verses to your teacher.
- Report to the cage ball. Roll the cage ball around the circle 10 times. Teammates should form a circle with their backs to the inside of the circle. Roll the ball around the outside.

MEMORY GAME WARM-UP
Grade Levels: 2-8

Equipment

- Music

Description and Setup

This activity serves the purpose as the motivator as well as the warm-up. The teacher starts the music and gives the students instruction in how to move around the gym—run, skip, gallop, walk, or hop. When the music stops, they find a person to high-five while saying their name. They have to remember that person as their high-five buddy. When the music starts again, they should begin moving in a different way, as instructed by the teacher. When the music stops, they need to find a handshake buddy with whom they will shake hands and say their name. Then they have to find their high-five buddy as well and give them another high-five. This could go on as long as the teacher would like. Each time the music stops, the students have to find a new buddy, do what the teacher instructs, then find all prior buddies in the correct order and perform the action they originally did together. Possible buddies could be elbow, hip, pinkie, and so on. As always, see if the students have any ideas for possible buddies, and let them take on the teacher role.

WINTER WONDERLAND WARM-UP
Grade Levels: 2-6

Equipment

- Music (if desired)

Description and Setup

Before the children enter the gym, the teacher posts signs at various stations in the gym, which have activities written on them. For instance, during the winter, the activities could be

- Jumping Jack Frost
- Polar Push-Ups
- Magic Mountain Climbers
- Snowflake Sit-Ups
- Blizzard Bounds
- Windy Windmills

After the motivator, while the students are sitting in their teams, talk about the four seasons and the type of winter you are currently having. Point out the six poster board stations located in the gym. Tell the students that once the music starts, the teams must stay together and move through the winter wonderland the way the teacher has asked them—for example, by skipping. Once the music stops, the team should report to a winter wonderland station and perform that activity until the music starts again. Each time the teams complete a station, the teacher could yell out a new way to move to the music. Teachers will need to stop and start the music a total of six times so that all teams can do all activities. Only one team can be at an activity at a time, and each must find an open station. The teacher can keep the music playing as long as necessary for the students to get a good workout.

FITNESS TAG

Grade Levels: 1-8

Equipment

- Pinnies or vests (6)
- Exercises (6)
- Jump ropes (6)

Description and Setup

Students report to the gym and sit in their teams. The teacher should select one team to be the taggers. The taggers should wear a colored vest or pinnie with an exercise taped to it. Examples of the exercises:

- Sit-ups (5)
- Push-ups (5)
- Jumping jacks (10)
- Windmills (10)
- Jump-rope jumps (10)
- Squat thrusts or burpees (5)

If the teacher would like to use music as a signal, the taggers would attempt to tag as many people as possible when the music starts. When tagged, that person must perform the exercise that is taped to the tagger's vest. After performing the activity, the student can reenter the game.

Variations

- Have all students gallop, skip, walk, and so on.
- Allow another team to be the taggers.

FOLLOW THE YELLOW BRICK ROAD
Grade Levels: K-6

Equipment

- Chairs (2)
- Tables (2)
- Cones (12)
- Small hurdles, 3-by-6-inch (6)

Description and Setup

This is our favorite warm-up, and it can be used many ways. The students do the warm-up after reporting to their teams. Or, once they know that the "road" is up, they can start walking on it as soon as they enter they gym. The road is the perimeter of the gym (figure 2.8). The gym should have a cone in each corner, set far enough away from a wall to allow students to pass safely between the cone and the wall. With music playing (optional), the students start walking along the road. After one or two laps, the teacher should give a signal to change the locomotor movement used to move on the road: skipping, sliding, galloping, jogging, running faster, running with a partner, running with your team, and so on. To make this warm-up even more fun, the teacher could have obstacles set up in the road the next time the students come to the gym. Examples of obstacles:

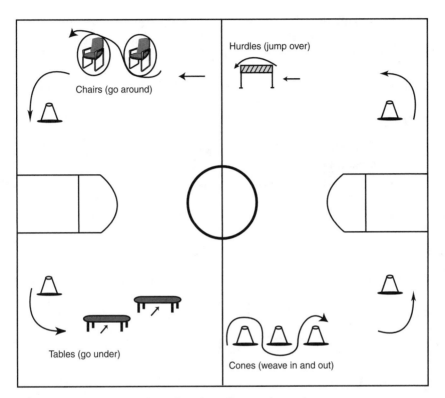

Chairs (go around)

Hurdles (jump over)

Tables (go under)

Cones (weave in and out)

Figure 2.8 Gym setup for Follow the Yellow Brick Road.

- Hurdles to jump over
- Tables to go under
- Cones to weave in and out
- Chairs to go around

Variations

- Place a different locomotor movement sign in each corner. Students have to move to the next corner according to the movement on that sign.

- Feed Tag: At one corner, place a stuffed animal (Tag). At the corner closest to Tag, place the animal's food (tennis balls, beanbags, or crumpled paper). The students should walk the first lap, grab one item of food, then follow the road to feed Tag. When they get to Tag's corner, they place the food in Tag's box and continue along the road. The teacher can change locomotor movements after each lap. The teacher may have to take some food out of Tag's box and put it back in the buckets to keep the feeding process going. See figure 2.9 for a diagram of Feed Tag.

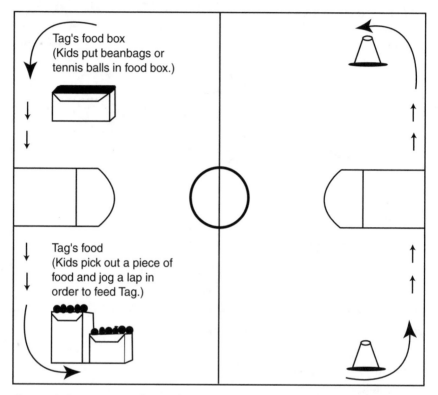

Figure 2.9 Gym setup for Feed Tag.

SAVE EASTER
Grade Levels: K-3

Equipment

- Small items, such as beanbags, tennis balls, crumpled paper, or shuttle-cocks (150)

Description and Setup

This is a great warm-up for younger children, and it can be done outdoors or in the gym. Each team needs a bucket or a box. The children on each team must run out into the field and bring back one "baby bunny" (the small items) and put it in the bucket before a storm comes and the baby bunnies can't find their way home. Each team should gather around their bucket or box. On the signal from the teacher, all team members must run out into the field and gather up a baby bunny. They must then run back and place it in their bucket or box. The team members continue until all baby bunnies are collected. Only one baby bunny can be brought back at a time. The farther away from the buckets, the greater the workout for the students.

The baby bunnies can be tennis balls, beanbags, crumpled paper, shuttlecocks, and so on. Each child should have at least five chances to save a bunny, so you will need a lot of bunnies. For a class of 30 students, you will need about 150 bunnies. The teacher should place all the bunnies in the field before the first class starts. After all the bunnies have been saved and are resting in their bucket or box, the students can take two or three and run out into the field and scatter the bunnies for the next class. See figure 2.10 for a diagram of Save Easter.

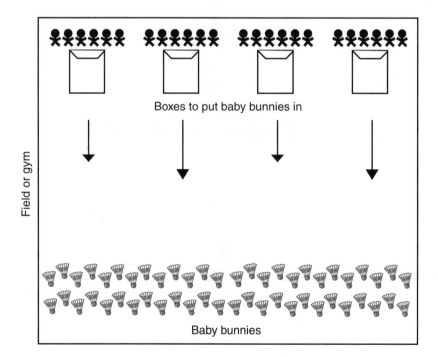

Figure 2.10 Gym setup for Save Easter.

VAULT TAG

Grade Levels: 1-8

Equipment

- Enough folded gym mats to divide the gym into quarters

Description and Setup

This is another warm-up that can be done in teams. The students can work together to set the mats up, take them down, and stack them after the game. It saves wear and tear on the teacher and gives the students an opportunity to assist the teacher as well as work cooperatively. After the teams do their team break, one student per team is chosen to be "It" and that student stays in place, giving the rest of the team time to scatter to another area of the gym. When the other students come to the mat and want to cross it to

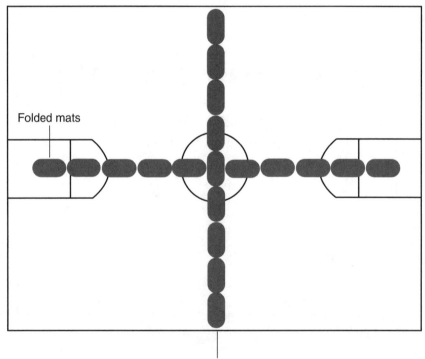

Folded mats

Folded mats

Figure 2.11 Gym setup for Vault Tag.

enter a new gym section, they must vault over the mat. Running on top of the mat is not allowed. A teacher may invoke the "your feet cannot touch a mat" rule, but keep in mind that a complete vault is difficult for young children. You may allow younger children to briefly touch the mat with their feet if they cannot get all the way over in one vault. The younger children should, however, attempt to put their weight on their hands as they push off with their feet. The teammate who is It can carry a tagger of some sort, such as a Frisbee, a small rubber ball, or a foam pin. On the signal from the teacher, the taggers try to tag a member of their team. Any player who is tagged becomes the new tagger, and the game continues. See figure 2.11 for a diagram of Vault Tag.

Variations

- Use two taggers from each team.
- Increase the height of the folded mats.
- Use different locomotor movements.
- Let one team be the taggers attempting to tag anyone on the other team. If tagged, a student must receive a high-five from a teammate to return to the game.

FOX AND GEESE
Grade Levels: 1-6

Equipment

- Snow
- Tagging frisbees (6)

Description and Setup

This game has been around for many years, and we have all probably played it at some time in our lives. For gym class, though, we would like to present it as a team warm-up or as a game students could play for the whole period. It would serve quite well as a warm-up to ice skating or sledding. The teacher will have to take some time in the morning to make four large diagrams in the snow.

Across both circles, draw two straight lines that intersect at the center. Where the lines touch the outer rim, there should be an area trampled out, marking the goose coop. There should be one less goose coop than there are geese, or two less goose coops per team. For a team of six, for example, there should be four coops and four geese, each goose occupying one coop; one goose is loose on the trail; and the fox is in its den in the center of the circle.

The object of this game is for the geese to run from coop to coop without being caught by the fox. The geese and the fox can only run on the trails (the lines of the diagram). The geese can run in any direction, on any line, at any time. When a fox tags a goose, the two exchange places. The fox becomes a goose, and the goose becomes a fox. The goose coops are "safe places"; that is, a goose cannot be tagged by a fox while in a coop. There is some risk involved in this game, as the geese should be encouraged to run to another coop using a route other than the outer rim. See figure 2.12 for a diagram of Fox and Geese.

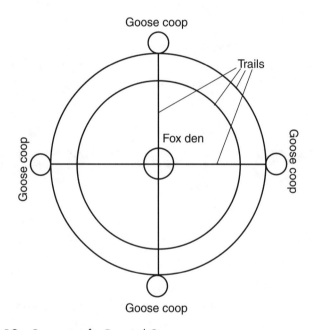

Figure 2.12 Gym setup for Fox and Geese.

Variations

A goose that occupies a coop must give it up when another goose arrives, provided the incoming goose asks for it politely. For example, "Excuse me, can I have this coop please?" or "Have a nice day. I need your coop." Put two teams together, make enough lines and dens, and the game will be more fun than ever.

TEAM CHOICE WARM-UP
Grade Levels: 1-8

Equipment

- None, unless a team requests some special items that day

Description and Setup

After the students have reported to their huddle, have all the teams jog two laps around the field or gym as one team to loosen up and get the blood flowing to the muscles. When the students return to their huddles, allow one team to lead a warm-up of their own creation. (Make sure to notify that team one week in advance so that students have time to prepare.) Teams could lead a series of exercises, and if they want to be more creative, use equipment and music. If your class has five teams and each team is responsible for three warm-ups during the semester, that's 15 days of warm-ups led by students. Team captains are responsible for communicating to the teacher the type of warm-ups being used. Be prepared for some imaginative warm-ups!

FOUR-CORNERS TEAM WARM-UP
Grade Levels: 1-8

Equipment

- None needed unless requested by students

Description and Setup

As the students report to their huddles, the teacher can direct them to a cone in one of the four corners of the gym. Once each team reaches their cone, have them count off one through six. Instruct all teams to do one lap around the perimeter of the gym. When they return to their corner, all the number 1s will select their favorite exercise, then lead their team in 10 repetitions of that exercise. After performing the activity, all the number 1s lead their teams in another lap around the gym. When they return, all the number 2s lead an exercise and a lap. This continues until all teammates have had a chance to lead an exercise and a lap.

Variations

- Add music.
- At each corner, do a skill that relates to the unit being taught. For example, for a basketball unit:

    a. Chest passes (10), one lap

    b. Bounce passes (10), one lap

    c. Pivots (10), one lap

    d. Layups (10), one lap

    e. Dribbles with each hand (10), one lap

- Add more laps between activities.
- Add equipment of various kinds in the center of the gym. The team captains can select the equipment needed for their exercises.

TEAM WARM-UP: LOCOMOTOR PARADE
Grade Levels: 1-6

Equipment

- None needed

Description and Setup

After the students have reported to their huddle, have each team line up in single file. When the signal is given (we like music), have the first student in line lead the team anywhere in the gym, doing a locomotor movement of choice. The rest of the team follows, copying the locomotor movement. When the teacher yells "Switch!" the student leading the line jogs to the back. The new leader of the line can now choose a new locomotor skill or continue with the old one. Continue this process until everyone has had a chance to lead the team.

Variations

- Add music.
- Provide obstacles in the gym to jump over, crawl under, or weave through.
- Use winter movements such as skating, skiing, or snowshoeing.

TEAM WARM-UP: ANIMAL ACTION
Grade Levels: K-3

Equipment

- Paper bags (1 per team)

- Animal pictures, or pieces of paper with animal names (at least 6 different animals, 1 for each team member)

Description and Setup

After the students have reported to their team huddle and have finished any huddle responsibilities for that day, direct each team to a corner of the gym. Give each team a paper bag with the names or pictures of six animals inside. On the signal, one team member reaches inside the bag and pulls out one animal. That person then leads the rest of the team in that animal movement for one lap. When the team returns to their bag, another student gets a chance to draw out an animal and lead the team. This process continues until all team members have had a chance to lead the team.

Variations

- Put enough animals in the bag for two turns for each teammate.
- Use music to add to this warm-up.
- Select animals that require fast movements.
- Allow students to use gym scooters for animals such as turtles and fish.

Suggested animals include the following:
- pony
- greyhound dog
- tiger
- cheetah
- rabbit
- frog
- kangaroo
- eagle

TEAM WARM-UP: FOREST ADVENTURE
Grade Levels: 1-5

Equipment

- None needed

Description and Setup

After the students have reported to their team huddle, ask them to name some items they may find in a forest. Possible answers you may get are branch, tree, log, bridge, and leaf. Select four items and ask the students to demonstrate with their bodies how they think these objects look. When a student happens upon the position you require for the game, have that student demonstrate the position for the class and let everyone practice it. When everyone is familiar with the way the object is portrayed in the forest, make up some rules for each object. For example:

- Tree: Stand straight and tall, with arms over your head. Action Rule: Run around tree.
- Branch: Stand straight, with arms spread wide apart and parallel to the ground. Action Rule: Duck under branch.
- Bridge: Bend forward and balance on toes and hands, with hips high enough for someone to crawl under. Action Rule: Crawl under bridge on tummy.
- Bush: Squat on floor, hugging knees. Action Rule: Skip around bush.
- Log: Lie flat on the floor, arms to sides. Action Rule: Jump over log.
- Rock: Lie on floor, on your side with knees to chest, arms hugging knees. Action Rule: Hop on one foot around rock.

Now let two teams portray the items in the forest. These two teams must spread out in the gym and try not to move once they are in position. On signal, the other two teams must run through the forest and perform the desired action when they come to a forest object. On signal—clap your hands, whistle, or just yell "Change!"—the students must alter the way they move through the forest but must keep the action rule the same. After two minutes, yell "Switch!" The forest objects now become forest adventurers, and the forest adventurers now become forest objects. Repeat this process until you think everyone has had a great workout.

Variations

- Use music while adventurers are moving through the forest.
- Change objects and action rules. Let students come up with more ideas.
- Put all the objects in a straight line—"a human forest obstacle course."

TEAM WARM-UP: PICK A CARD
Grade Levels: 1-8

Equipment

- None needed unless some of the variations are attempted.

Description and Setup

As the students report to their team huddle, each captain is given a card with a locomotor skill on it. On the teacher's signal, the team performs that locomotor skill, moving wherever they please—as a team—throughout the gym. When the teacher signals again, the captains for that day exchange cards, and the team performs the new locomotor movement. This continues until all teams have performed all locomotor movements.

Variations

- Add music.
- Add a locomotor skill plus an exercise on the card, such as push-ups.
- Add equipment. For example, the card might say, "Skip until the teacher's whistle, then get a volleyball and do 20 serves to a partner."

TEAM WARM-UP: LEADER OF THE PACK
Grade Levels: 1-8

Equipment

- None needed unless variations are used.

Description and Setup

After students report to their team huddle, the teacher or captain assigns a locomotor movement to each member of the team. For example,

- Teammate number 1: Walk
- Teammate number 2: Jog
- Teammate number 3: Run
- Teammate number 4: Skip
- Teammate number 5: Gallop
- Teammate number 6: Jump

Other movements could include hop, leap, slide, walk backward, gallop with opposite foot leading, and so on.

When the teacher gives the signal, teammates number 1 leads their teams around the gym, doing the assigned locomotor movement. After about 30 to 50 seconds, the teacher should blow a whistle, bang a drum, or just yell "Change!" On this signal, the leader goes to the back of the line, and now teammates number 2 are in the front. The teams follow their new leader and do the new locomotor movement. Each leader is free to move anywhere in the gym, with the team behind them. Each teammate should get a chance to lead.

Variations

- Add music.
- Add equipment. For example, you can add a basketball and arrange the game as follows:

  Teammate number 1 leads 30 seconds of jogging and 60 seconds of chest passing.

  Teammate number 2 leads 30 seconds of jumping and 60 seconds of bounce passing.

  Teammate number 3 leads 30 seconds of skipping and 60 seconds of dribbling.

  Teammate number 4 leads 30 seconds of galloping and 60 seconds of layups.

  Teammate number 5 leads 30 seconds of running and 60 seconds of pivots and stretching.

  Teammate number 6 leads 30 seconds of walking and 60 seconds of ball handling.

SHADOW TAG
Grade Levels: K-6

Equipment

- Overhead projectors

Description and Setup

This warm-up should be played outdoors on a sunny day. Each team plays against their own teammates with one teammate being "It." When the person who is It steps on a teammate's shadow and yells the shadow owner's name, that shadow owner then becomes It. A great variation is to put four overheads in a gym, with each team being assigned one overhead. The shadows are displayed on the wall, and the It would have to tag a shadow with the hand and yell the tagged person's name. When tagged, that person becomes the new It. Give each team one half of the wall, and arrange the overhead to illuminate that wall. Turn down the lights and have fun.

OVERHEAD OBSTACLE COURSE WARM-UP
Grade Levels: 1-8

Equipment

- Overhead projectors (3 or 4)

Description and Setup

Arrange the overheads so that one entire wall is lit up and will show the students' shadows. Arrange dimes or draw dots on the glass plate of the overhead so that the shadows of the dimes and dots will show up on the wall. Place the dots at different heights. Students (and their shadows) can then jump over, duck under, jump and touch, or crawl under the shadow obstacles. Let the students run one at a time the entire length of the wall, maneuvering their shadows through the obstacle course. Five or six students can attempt the course at once, provided that they are spaced out evenly. See figure 2.13 for a diagram of Overhead Obstacle Course Warm-Up.

Variations

- Try the obstacle course while dribbling a ball.

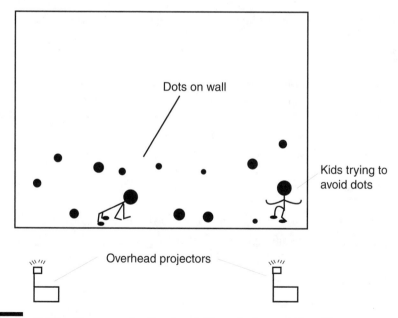

Figure 2.13 Gym setup for Overhead Obstacle Course Warm-Up.

- Try the obstacle course while connected to a teammate.
- All six teammates go through the course without letting go of hands.

MATH RACE WARM-UP
Grade Levels: 1-8

Equipment

- Cones, or markers of some sort (30)

Description and Setup

Put the cones in a straight line about five feet apart on a field or in the gym. Tell the students to listen carefully to your story, as they must mathematically figure out the answer as you tell the story. The students should be in their team huddles near the starting line. The story can sound something like this.

Teams: Run the length of 29 cones. Step backward 5 cones (24). Skip 6 cones forward (30). Run to the halfway point (15). Gallop 5 cones forward (20) and do 10 push-ups. Subtract 11 cones (9) and slide to that cone. Do 20 sit-ups, now sprint forward twice that distance. Where do you end up? (18th cone)

When the students have figured out the answer in their teams, they must do the actions in the story. Which team can get to the correct cone the quickest?

Variations

- Give students several math problems like this one on a sheet of paper. Put the music on, and let them do all the problems in a row. Great workout!
- Add higher math functions for older students.
- Even if one team starts before other teams, that may not necessarily mean they have the correct answer. Encourage all teams to finish the problem and do the warm-up.

DODGING WARM-UP
Grade Levels: K-6

Equipment

- A gym or outlined field
- Music (optional)

Description and Setup

After greeting the students and reporting them to their teams, start a short discussion about the meaning of *dodging*. Let the students offer their opinions on the meaning before you tell them yours. The meaning should, however, end up something like this: "Changing directions quickly to avoid a collision." Now challenge the students with the following dodging challenge: "Who thinks they can move around the gym and not touch anyone else? Remember, you have to dodge to avoid a collision." Now give them the following rule: Whenever the teacher yells "Change!" they have to find a new locomotor movement to use, and they have to change speed and direction. For example, "You may be doing a slow walk, but when I yell 'Change!' you might do a fast run in the opposite direction."

Now put the music on and let the students move around the gym. After several "changes," stop them and challenge them to do the exact same thing, but just use one-half of the gym. (It is much harder to dodge now.) After several minutes of half-court, try the same routine on one-fourth of the court. Finally, put all the students inside the basketball free throw lane and watch the effort put forth in attempting to avoid touching someone else. Remember to keep challenging them. The kids love this warm-up, and you can follow it with a good discussion on how hard it is to dodge. This was the first warm-up I did as a teacher in 1967.

7 JUMPS WARM-UP
Grade Levels: K-5

Equipment

- Music: "7 Jumps" tape or CD

Description and Setup

The song "7 Jumps" has been around for ages. It was old when I started in 1967, and again, this warm-up is one of the first I ever used. The song is a lively folk-dance rhythm that is interrupted by a series of "beeps." When the music is playing, let the kids move around the gym—however the music makes them feel. When the beeps sound, instruct them to do the following: first beep, lie on belly; second beep, lie on back; third beep, kneel on knees. When the music starts again, continue moving around the gym. The beeps continue, and each time they sound, there will be one more added. Keep the rotation of belly, back, and knees throughout the song. It is a great warm-up.

Variations

- Do an exercise, such as push-ups or sit-ups, during each beep.
- Change locomotor movements during the music.

POP GOES THE WEASEL
Grade Levels: K-5

Equipment

- Music: "Pop Goes the Weasel"

Description and Setup

Let the children move about the gym as the music is being played. Designate a movement, or let them move however the music makes them feel. On the first "pop," each child must perform an exercise until the next "pop," at which time they must change exercises. Continue this sequence until the record is over.

Variations

- Let a different student lead everyone each time there is a "pop."
- Let the students run around the gym, and every time there is a "pop," they must jump high, then continue running.
- Every time there is a "pop," the students must change the way they move.

SLOW TO FAST WARM-UP
Grade Levels: K-5

Equipment

- A record player (yes, a record player) and an old record (45, 33, or 78 rpm)

Description and Setup

One neat thing a record player can do that a CD cannot do is change speeds. This is an old warm-up I used when I first started teaching and when record players were our source of music. Discuss with the students the different speeds they could do while moving in the gym. They should come up with *slow* (33 rpm), *medium-fast* (45 rpm), and *faster* (78 rpm). Put the record on the correct speed, and let the students move around the gym using any type of movement they wish. After several minutes, change speed of the record player. For example, if you have a 45 rpm record, switch it to 33 while it is playing. When this happens, the students must change the speed of their movement to match the speed of the music. Challenge them to see how slowly they can move or how quickly and carefully when the music switches to 78 rpm. A great warm-up!

Variations

- Make the kids change the way they move every time you switch speeds.

- Try to do a sports skill to the speed of the record—for example, passing a football.

CHARACTER-EDUCATION TREASURE HUNT
Grade Levels: 3-8

Equipment

- Index cards (36; 6 colors, 6 index cards per color)
- Boxes or buckets (6)
- Paper and pencil (for each team)

Description and Setup

Divide the index cards evenly among six different colors (or six index cards per color). Each card should contain a character-education term, as well as a point value and an activity. Use the character-education words listed in this chapter, or make up your own with some new terms. All of the cards should be hidden around the gym, and the six boxes or buckets should be placed in a circle in the middle of the gym. Students should be in their teams, with each team assigned a bucket or box. One student from each team is assigned the role of the hunter. On the signal from the teacher, the teams start jogging around the perimieter of the gym. On the second signal from the teacher, the hunter ventures away from the team in search of a character-education card. When the hunters find a card, they must call the team to that spot, and everyone must perform the activity on that card. The hunter then takes the card and puts it in the team's bucket.

When the hunters successfully place the card in the bucket, they rejoin their teams, which continue to jog around the gym. When each hunter gets back to the team, a new hunter ventures forth, looks for a new card, and the process continues. The game ends when all six cards have been placed in the bucket and when the team figures out the correct point value of all the cards. Wouldn't it be great to hear the teams yelling to the hunter, "We need *Respect*! Find *Respect*!" For an example of a character education card, see figure 2.14.

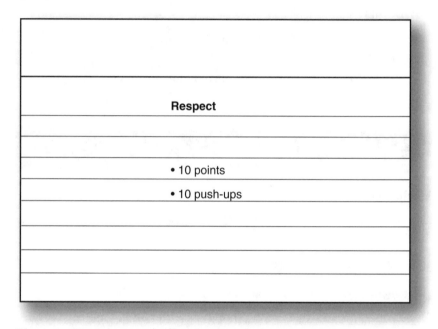

Respect

- 10 points
- 10 push-ups

Figure 2.14 Respect character education card.

Variations

- Hide the cards under mats, pins, balls, bases, poly spots, and so on. This makes the game more exciting by testing the students' memories; they have to remember where their teammates looked so that they don't revisit the same spots.

- Mathematics: Give each team a paper and pencil. The team must show their addition work at the end of the game. For older kids, use multiplication and division on the cards. Figure out ways to challenge them.

INTEGRITY TOWER: FITNESS RELAY
Grade Levels: 1-8

Equipment

- Foam blocks (24)
- Folded gym mat (1)
- Gym scooters (2 per team)
- Spot markers, or bases (3 per team)

Description and Setup

The foam blocks used in this game are actually character-education blocks. Divide the foam blocks into four sets of six. Each block must have a character-education word printed on them: *Respect, Character, Sportspersonship, Judgment, Pride, Integrity.* Using the blocks, students work together to plan and build a tower by transporting the blocks in relay fashion to the building site. This activity enhances physical fitness, teamwork, and a clear understanding of the importance of good values.

Teammates number 1, the character-education blocks, and the folded mat should be at station 1, at one end of the gym. When the teacher gives the signal to begin, teammates number 1 each place one of the character-education blocks on the folded mat and push the mat ("transport the block") to station 2, which should be one-quarter the length of the gym away from station 1. Station 2 should have teammates number 2 and a gym scooter. When teammate number 1 arrives at station 2, teammates number 2 take the character-education block, sit on the gym scooter, and transport the block to teammates number 3, who are waiting at station 3, which is at the half-court line (or halfway between the start and finish).

Teammates number 3 must wait until the block arrives by gym scooter. Upon arrival from teammates number 2, they take the brick and transport it via the second gym scooter, delivering it to teammates number 4, who are waiting at the next station, three-fourths the length of the gym away from station 1. Teammates number 4 wait at their base at station 4. When the block arrives, teammates number 4 take it and sprint to the building site, which is located at the end of the gym. When the block arrives at the building site, teammates number 4 should start constructing the integrity tower. After delivering a block, all teammates must return to their original station, traveling back in the same fashion and waiting for the next block. Teammates number 1 get the best workout, as they will be pushing a folded mat back and forth many times. The team that can build the tower the

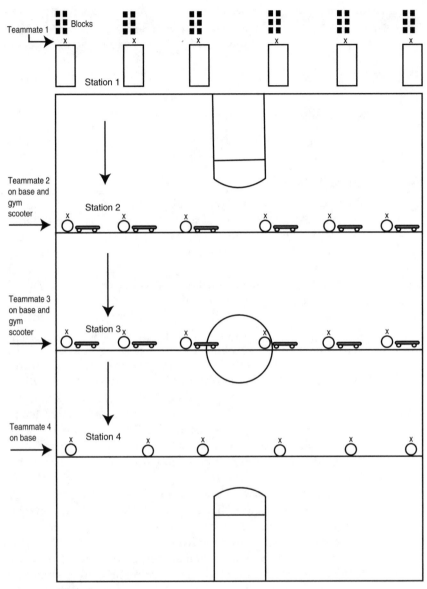

Teammate 1 → Blocks

Station 1

Teammate 2
on base and
gym
scooter →

Station 2

Teammate 3
on base and
gym
scooter →

Station 3

Teammate 4
on base →

Station 4

Building site

Figure 2.15 Gym setup for Integrity Tower: Fitness Relay.

quickest wins the relay. See figure 2.15 for a diagram of Integrity Tower: Fitness Relay.

Teacher hints: Use this opportunity to discuss what it takes to build an integrity tower. Tell the kids that they can shape their character using these same "building blocks."

Additions and Variations

- Build the tower as high as possible—the team with the highest tower wins rather than the one with the fastest-built tower.
- Use some other items to help build the tower, such as beanbags, balls, or rhythm sticks. Label these *Dishonesty*, *Cheating*, and *Greed*. See what happens when you add these items to your tower. Is it easier or harder to build an integrity tower using these values? Should you use these blocks to build your life?
- Find different ways to move the block from station to station. Use different locomotor movements or vehicles, such as a pulling a tire with the block on it, performing a forward roll, or swinging on a rope. Be creative.
- Rotate stations so that every child gets a chance to build a tower.
- The team should plan in a huddle what order the blocks will be delivered.

TEAM-TOSS TAG
Grade Levels: 1-12

Equipment

- Foam balls, 5 or 6 inches (3)
- A gym, or large playing area that can be divided into sections
- Colored vests, or pinnies (6)

Description and Setup

We love this warm-up—it's a tagging game, born in a college education class, where the students really had a great time playing it. This tagging game has it all: passing, catching, teamwork, strategy, dodging, and running. For this warm-up, you can divide the gym into as many sections as there are members on one team. This description uses a team of six.

Divide the gym into six sections. Place a tagger in each section, each wearing a colored vest. The taggers cannot leave their sections. The rest of the students can move freely, anywhere they want to avoid a tag. The taggers can only tag people in their section, and they can only tag with a foam ball.

To start the game, give two foam balls to the taggers. As the students flee the sections to avoid a tag, the taggers must pass the ball to their team-mate taggers in the other sections to tag a student. Once tagged, the student must freeze, and to reenter the game, he or she has to receive a high-five from another student. See figure 2.16 for a diagram of Team Toss Tag.

Variations

- Add or reduce tagger sections.
- Add more balls.
- Use bigger balls, and make the area smaller for young kids.
- Consider using a football field and with foam footballs (instead of regular foam balls).

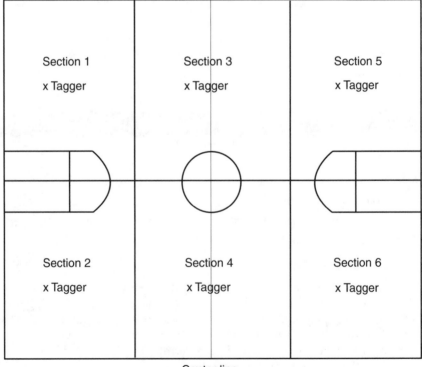

Center line

Figure 2.16 Gym setup for Team Toss Tag.

TEAM WARM-UP: TEAM-TAG COMPETITION
Grade Levels: 1-8

Equipment

- Colored vests or pinnies, enough for each member of one team

Description and Setup

After the teams have met in their huddles and have had their huddle break, designate one team to be "It." The boundaries for this game are inside the basketball court, but there should also be an area outside the court for walking. The team that is appointed as It should put on the pinnies. This team is timed to see how many seconds/minutes it takes them to tag all the other students. Upon saying "Go!" the teacher starts the watch, then stops it when the last person is tagged. When a student gets tagged, they immediately go to the outside of the court and start walking the perimeter. As soon as the last person is tagged, the next team puts on the pinnies, and the game starts again. This continues until all teams have had a chance to be It. After the last team has tagged everyone, the teams should high-five each other for a competitive warm-up well played.

While this is an elimination game, which in most cases is taboo, the students do keep moving after being tagged and are only out for a short while. You can even have them jump rope after being tagged, or play catch, or something else creative.

This is a very competitive warm-up, as each team is trying to get the best time. For additional safety, give the members of the tagging team a nerf ball to use as a tagger.

Variations

- Try this game using different locomotor movements, such as skipping or galloping.

TEAM WARM-UP: SPORTS MOBILE
Grade Levels: 1-6

Equipment

- Sport music: "Jock Jams" or some other lively music

Description and Setup

Assign each team a sport. For four teams of six, the sports could be basketball, football, softball, and volleyball. Now each team should identify six skills related to their sport. The teacher may have to show these skills to the younger children. For basketball, the skills could be jump shot, rebound, dribble, pass, defensive slide, and free throw. For football: hiking, blocking, punting, passing, receiving, and carrying the ball through tacklers. For softball: batting, pitching, throwing from center field, stretching to make the catch on first base, fielding a ground ball at shortstop and throwing to first, and bunting. For volleyball: bumping, overhead pass, serve, spike, block, dig, and roll. Each child in each team should be assigned a skill for their team's sport. When the music starts, each team's sports mobile will start. Each skill must be acted out as though they are playing in a championship game. When the teacher momentarily stops the music, each team member takes a new skill and acts it out when the teacher starts the music again. Continue until every team member has acted out all of their assigned sport skills. Encourage the teams to really get into it. They should pretend this is an important game, and they should do the skills as hard as possible.

Variations

- Make this a long warm-up, and have each team do each sport.
- Have the team sports mobile be physically connected somehow so that everyone must work as a team.
- Have the teams line up in a straight line with each student performing a skill one at a time. Keep repeating, and work toward a smooth-running mobile.
- Try videotaping their sports mobile movements, and play back for the class.

More Ways to Keep the Focus on Character

Buy and mark playground balls with the character-education focus words listed in this book. The kids can then play four-square, kick ball, or any other game with balls that are marked with words such as *Sportspersonship*, *Tolerance*, or *Pride*. This would be one way to keep the focus on these words and further impress their meaning upon the students.

Other types of equipment we could mark with character-education words:

- Cones
- Bats
- Beanbags

- Signs in the gym
- Teachers, be creative! Find ways to keep these words in focus the entire year.

Students make a powerful emotional connection to their teammates when this daily ritual has been created. Through chapter 1, we established how important it is to make an emotional connection; through chapter 2, we provided specific techniques to further create community and develop character. To continue this connection, we recommend participating in a one-week team-building unit, about the third week of school, after teams have constructed their team pacts. This activity enables the students to physically and emotionally support one another and further strengthen their relationships. Also, by doing this soon after teams have been developed, students can have the opportunity to practice the concepts of praise and encouragement. We continue this line of thought in the next chapter by providing different team-building challenges and the specific details to facilitate the process.

Team Building

Team building is the cooperative process that a group uses to solve both physical and mental challenges. While using this process and solving the challenges, the group learns how to share ideas, praise and encourage one another, physically and emotionally support one another, and (slowly) start becoming a team.

The purpose of this chapter is to continue forming and solidifying the team's connection initiated in the huddle activities. The next step is to provide opportunities that help the students work together and use the social skills they have learned. The opportunities that continue this connection are the team-building challenges. In this chapter, we provide 20 new challenges for you and your students, and in addition, you will learn:

- How relationship-driven teaching is similar to team building
- How team building affects self-esteem
- What roles are needed to do team building properly
- When to use positive adjectives

Team building is the one method used in physical education today that comes the closest to providing a nonthreatening, peer-supportive environment for students. Some of us were fortunate enough to be on a supportive athletic team while growing up. One of the rewards of being on that team was the memories it created. The struggles, failures, and eventual success brought a lot of satisfaction to our lives.

Team building in the physical education setting gives all children a chance to be both supportive of and supported by teammates in physical education, regardless of their athletic skill or inclination.

The concept of team building was introduced into the physical education world in Minnesota in 1992. The philosophy behind this concept is that while struggling to solve a challenge, kids can learn how to be good teammates. Team building forces students to exchange ideas and work together to solve a problem. They learn to listen to one another, deal with failures, and persevere as a team. While being a member of a team, kids learn that when they solve a challenge, it is better to cooperate and offer one another both physical and emotional support. Throughout each challenge, kids learn to value teamwork. They learn to brainstorm solutions, develop a plan of attack, and praise and encourage teammates along the way. Team building is included in this book because it provides kids with a connection to a team—a connection many of us can remember from our athletic years.

Key Terms

- Relationship-driven teaching
- Team building and the development of self-esteem
- Team-building roles

    Organizer

    Praiser

    Encourager

- Positive adjectives

Relationship-Driven Teaching

One of the best articles written in the past few years concerning making connections to student's emotional needs was written by Spence Rogers and Lisa Renard (1999). Published in *Educational Leadership* magazine, this article was titled "Relationship-Driven Teaching." In it, they suggest that teachers can motivate students when they fulfill the students' fundamental emotional needs by creating meaningful relationships among the students. "When we develop one-on-one relationship skills—becoming aware of and tending to the emotional needs of students—we enter the realm of learning as well. If learning in school meets students' emotional needs, they will more likely engage in the learning."

In fact, because physical educators have been so concentrated on meeting students' physical needs, maybe they have overlooked the students' emotional side. We often push students to become more active, and we are constantly on the lookout for new and fun motivation methods to accomplish our fitness goals and keep students active. Thus, in our efforts to get kids fit, we may not be approaching our goals from the right perspective. Rogers and Renord feel that students must ". . . value the activities enough to want to learn and achieve. Learning occurs only when what is being presented is meaningful enough to the student that he or she decided to actively engage in the learning experience."

This article was written for the academic classroom teacher; however, the philosophy behind the article is also appropriate for physical education. In particular, Rogers and Renord give us a framework of six standards that help fulfill emotional needs and build motivation. Let's apply these standards to team building and see if they fit.

Standard Number One: Safe

For students to place priority on learning, they must feel safe from both physical danger and embarrassment.

Rogers and Renard

Certainly, team building in the PE setting falls within the context of the safety standard. There is some physical risk involved in team building, especially in the advanced challenges, but students can decide whether to take that risk or not. If they decide to attempt a new skill, they know that their teammates are supporting them and are with them during the attempt. If they succeed, the entire team rejoices, and each student may feel an increase in motivation for obtaining new skills. If they fail, they may (with the team's support) try again or move on to another challenge.

Eliminating criticism that stems from a student's lack of skill, either from a teacher or from peers, is constantly emphasized. The rules of team building are enforced, and the rules say, "no put-downs or negative pressure." Indeed, team building is all about emotional support, as well as physical support.

Standard Number Two: Valuable

Students are more apt to engage fully and produce quality work if they perceive that what they are doing has value.

Rogers and Renard

Each team member, during the course of a challenge, must actively engage in solving the challenge. They may give physical assistance or engage in brainstorming a solution. Doing advanced challenges especially requires physical assistance from team members. For example, helping someone negotiate a raging river or navigate down the side of a jagged mountain can be very rewarding. If each student actively helps solve the challenge and if the team is successful, each student's sense of value will be improved because every teammate will have had a chance to have input into a solution.

Imagine how you would feel if the team used your idea and solved the challenge. Imagine how you would feel if you successfully helped someone balance on a tire while trying to cross the river. In both these situations, students would perceive that what they accomplished had value.

Standard Number Three: Successful

To maintain intrinsic motivation students need evidence of success in achieving either mastery or significant progress toward mastery.

Rogers and Renard

During team building, teams can see and be involved in gradual completion of the challenge. For example, when students attempt to cross a river, help one another scale a mountain, or figure out a tough math puzzle, they can see physical progress being made. Even when teams encounter setbacks and penalties, students' enthusiasm rises as solutions become clearer. Again, team building fills this standard of success very well.

Standard Number Four: Involving

Students want to contribute and to participate if they have helped plan, administer, and make meaningful decisions about what and how they are learning.

Rogers and Renard

While solving a challenge, students are encouraged to listen to one another and evaluate opinions and ideas. A central part of relationship-based teaching is that students need to know that their ideas count. Even if some students are quiet and prefer not to contribute ideas, they too can feel like part of the solution when they help implement a teammate's idea and it results in success. If they are successful while complimenting a teammate, then even the quietest of students deserve a well-earned high-five or pat on the back. In fact, as they begin to feel more attached to the team, these quiet, shy students just may start to take more risks with the team's encouragement and support. Team building meets standard four quite well.

Standard Number Five: Caring

> Students respond positively to being liked and to being accepted
> and respectful members of the class. They want to be part of the
> group rather than outsiders.
>
> *Rogers and Renard*

Certainly this standard is what team building is about. Feeling like an accepted and valued member of the team is paramount to group problem
solving. Being praised and encouraged by team members certainly shows
they care about your success.

There are many challenges that require group physical effort and coor-
dination, and they all serve as opportunities to enhance caring. For example, the challenge Bridge Over the Raging River is much easier when all
students on the team help one another balance. If I help you physically and
you are successful because of my help, it will be a very satisfying feeling
for me. I will feel like part of a team effort. This is a no-brainer—team building fits.

Standard Number Six: Enabling

> Brain compatible, research-supported teaching techniques allow
> students to move around the classroom, address multiple modes
> of learning, acknowledge outlets for creative presentation of learn-
> ing, provide enough contrast to preclude boredom, and contrib-
> ute to a motivating context.
>
> *Rogers and Renard*

Many team-building activities have creative story lines. Creativity allows
students to become more motivated and less inhibited when they believe
there are "alligators in the river" or "electric fences on the bridge." Story
lines can add challenges. For example, "Can the team make it across this
narrow bridge that is suspended over the deep gorge before the storm
comes?" Story lines allow students to engage in the creativity, and it certainly adds excitement to a challenge.

Team building is a "best practice," (www.bpeducation.org) and it allows
for many types of active learning during the challenge process. If you haven't
tried team building, many new team-building challenges are offered in this
chapter. Also, *Team Building Through Physical Challenges* (Glover and Midura
1992) and *More Team Building Challenges* (Midura and Glover 1995), combined with this book, will give you over 50 challenges to choose from.

Team Building and Self-Esteem

The authors of *Team Building* wrote that a student's self-confidence grows as teams successfully master challenges. When it was written in 1992, the authors naturally assumed that this statement was true. In 1998, a study was conducted by Vicki Ebbock (Oregon State University) and Sandra Gibbons (University of Victoria) and was subsequently published in the *Journal of Sport and Exercise Physiology*. Through a physical challenges program, this study investigated the effectiveness of team building on the self-conceptions of physical education students in grades six and seven. The treatment group was exposed to one team-building activity every second week for eight months while the control group completed the regular physical education curriculum without any team-building activities. The results revealed that both male and female students in the team-building group were significantly higher than the control group on perceptions of self-worth, athletic competence, physical appearance, and social acceptance. Female students in the team-building group were also significantly higher on perceptions of scholastic competence and behavioral conduct than were female students in the control group. The original statement published in 1992 was thus proven to be accurate in 1998—no longer was it merely an assumption. Students were truly starting to connect to team building.

Earn Your Self-Esteem

One reason team building has become such a useful tool in building self-esteem is that, through it, children are not handed success—they have to earn it. The challenges become increasingly more difficult as the team moves through the sequence of beginning to advanced challenges. More often than not, a team fails in its pursuit of a solution. Frustration may start to show up within various team members. For example, many of the challenges require the team to start over if a rule is broken. The team must reorganize, try new solutions, support one another, and eventually solve the challenge.

Students have to remember that team building is a cooperative process, and many times during that process, failure may happen. When it does, teams may encounter frustration and not completely concentrate on solving the problem. In other cases, that failure may cause some teams to concentrate harder, cooperate more fully, and eventually solve the problem. Regardless, students learn that failure and struggle only make the eventual victory that much sweeter. Sometimes students need to fail in order to learn. Repeated failures often lead us to greater satisfaction when we eventually do succeed.

Lillian Katz, professor of early childhood education at the University of Illinois and former president of the National Association for the Education of Young Children, seems to agree. In her article "All About Me" (1993) in *American Educator* magazine, she describes the importance of young children's developing a positive self-image. In particular, the following quotes from her article are supportive of team building.

- "Self-esteem is likely to be fostered when children have challenging opportunities to build self-confidence and esteem through effort, persistence and the gradual accrual of skills, knowledge and appropriate behavior."

- "Cheap success in a succession of trivial tasks most likely will not foster self-esteem. Young children are more apt to benefit from real challenges and hard work than from frivolous one shot activities."

- "When children are engaged in challenging and significant activities, they are bound to experience some failures, reverses, and rebuffs. Children are able to cope with rebuffs, disappointments and failures when adults acknowledge and accept their feelings of discouragement and at the same time tell children they can try another time."

- "Learning to deal with setbacks and maintaining the persistence and optimism necessary for childhood's long and gradual road to mastery: these are the real foundations of lasting self-esteem."

Thus, the team-building philosophy seems to follow Ms. Katz's philosophy. It strengthens the need for physical educators to embrace team building as one way to get students to earn their self-esteem, gain confidence, and further connect with physical education.

Tolerance

One of the behaviors that schools have the most difficulty fostering in their students is the concept of respecting those who are different. Difference can encompass gangs rivaling other gangs and cliques antagonizing one another, but it can also be as small as one student's appearing nerdy to other students or simply having a disability.

Physical education can help the school a great deal when teaching about tolerance. Students have a wide variety of physical skills, and students who are highly skilled must learn to cooperate with and support those who are less skilled.

Team building provides an excellent resource for physical education, as put-downs and negative pressure are not allowed during the completion of a challenge. Teammates must learn to praise, encourage, and physically support other teammates. At the end of a series of challenges, teams do what are called *positive adjectives*. Teammates must pick three positive adjectives off a sheet that best describes the team member sitting in front of them. It is very hard to get upset with someone who has just said something nice to you. Discussing character-building words in either a large group or small group also goes a long way toward developing a kinder atmosphere and caring, tolerant attitude in physical education class.

The First Unit of the Year

As we said in the preceding chapter, a team-building unit of one or two weeks (depending on how often your classes meet) would be the next logical step. We feel that each team should get the opportunity to work together and complete about four to six beginning challenges. We encourage you not to do more than this because we do want your students to get involved in your traditional fall units.

Now pick out some beginning challenges—pick them from this book, or look at *Team Building Through Physical Challenge* and *More Team Building*. As beginning challenges, try Dynamic Barrier, Magic Bases, Geo Sphere, Coconut Collection, and Great Pearl Caper (from this chapter).

After two or three units of study within your curriculum, do another team-building unit that consists of both beginning challenges and intermediate challenges. You may want to do one more team-building unit toward the end of the winter before going back outside. This time select challenges that are much more difficult for your students.

Team building can be done anytime during the year. Some teachers have told us that when they notice that the attitude of the class breaks down from being respectful competitors to one of grumbling and poor sporting behavior, they will do a week of team building to get the good attitude back. The only rule we feel you should follow is to do team building as your first unit; after that, put it back into the curriculum whenever you would like.

Team-Building Roles

The process of team building requires several unique roles. In the following sections, we cover each in detail.

Organizer

When the team approaches a challenge, they see two cards: an organizer card and a challenge card.

These cards can be located in the appendix; laminate them and place each card at the appropriate challenge. The appointed organizer should pick up the challenge card and read it to the team. The challenge card lists the necessary equipment, the challenge description, and the rules and consequences of the challenges.

The organizer card includes questions that the organizer asks team members to help them understand each challenge. A team cannot start a challenge until it can answer all questions correctly. Good organizers do their best to communicate the challenge to the group, and they do not chastise the group if they cannot answer all the questions. The role of organizer should be rotated after each challenge. If some students do not want to be organizers, do not force them to fill this role. Use only the students that would prefer it. Some children may have reading problems, and this role could be very embarrassing to them.

Praiser

In the last chapter, learning how to praise and encourage was the first huddle activity; now they must put the practice of using praise phases to a test. Before the completion of the challenge, the praiser should find at least one specific act to praise. For example, if a teammate makes a good suggestion or helps another student balance, the praiser should acknowledge that act. Using specific praise phrases that the team practiced in their huddle is what the praiser should use. A good praiser is not phony when praising someone but sincere as possible.

The role of praiser should be rotated as the team moves through the challenges. Every teacher can secretly hope that everyone will start praising before long and that the role of praiser can be eliminated altogether.

Encourager

An encourager also acknowledges effort. An encourager must use positive encouragement while a teammate is attempting a challenge. Many times, this role may overlap that of the praiser. As with the praiser, the role of encourager may be eliminated as the team works through challenges. A good encourager uses the encouraging words practiced during the first huddle activity. If teammates should fail at a certain challenge, the encourager should let them know that the team is supporting them and that "you will get it next time; don't give up."

Positive Adjectives

At the completion of the team-building unit, teachers can use an activity called *positive adjectives*. Teams sit in a semicircle, with one team member

Positive adjectives		
Kind	Energetic	Determined
Neat	Organized	Convincing
Strong	Courageous	Content
Quiet	Honest	Sensible
Nice	Clever	Creative
Shy	Inventive	Independent
Happy	Imaginative	Determined
Active	Reserved	Humorous
Cheerful	Enthusiastic	Pleasant
Courteous	Helpful	Delightful
Intelligent	Aggressive	Calm
Polite	Bright	Confident
Friendly	Thoughtful	Daring

Figure 3.1 Positive adjectives.

sitting in front, facing teammates. Each team member should have a copy of positive adjectives (figure 3.1).

One by one, teammates look at the person sitting at the front of the semicircle and pick three positive adjectives that best describe that person. For example, "Chris, you are clever, daring, and courageous." Upon hearing these three adjectives, Chris should respond with a "thank you." The purpose of positive adjectives is to build a closer connection with your teammates. It is not easy to say something nice to a teammate when you are in middle school, and it is especially not easy to sit in front of a group and hear something nice being said about you. But, hopefully, this experience can foster a closer relationship among team members that can carry over into other aspects of their school day.

Team-Building Challenges

In our first team-building book, *Team Building Through Physical Challenges*, there are nine introductory team-building challenges, and in our second team-building book, *More Team Building Challenges*, there are five introductory challenges. The first challenge we present in this book is an example of an introductory challenge. The second and third challenges, though, are examples of intermediate and advanced challenges. These challenges are three of the most popular challenges from the other two team-building books. Following these three examples are brand new challenges we think you will really enjoy.

WHOLE WORLD

This challenge was featured in *Team Building Through Physical Challenges* (Glover and Midura 1992). It is one of the most popular challenges we do at workshops and in service presentations, but in this book, we are going to change it to make it even better.

Description

This is an introductory challenge. As in all challenges, group discussion should precede any physical attempt. In this challenge, the group is forced to solve a problem, but they need to figure out what their first attempt at solving the problem will be before they actually execute any steps so that the potential solution is understood by every teammate.

In this introductory challenge, physical assistance is not necessary, but you will notice the team working together to balance the ball. There are many ways to solve this challenge, and I am sure you will see smiles on the faces of students as they work together to solve the whole world. For this challenge, the group stands around a cage ball while it sits on a tire. A second tire should be resting on the floor, close to one-half the length of the gym away. Each team must figure out how to transport this ball while following the rules of the challenge.

Success Criteria

The challenge is mastered when the students successfully move the cage ball back and forth, from tire to tire, for a total of four trips.

Equipment

- Cage ball, 42 inches or larger (1)
- Tires (2)

Setup

You will need an open space, at least one-half the length of a basketball court. Set the large ball on one tire, and place the other tire about 40 to 50 feet away.

Rules and Sacrifices

- The cage ball cannot touch the floor.
- The cage ball cannot touch arms or hands of any group member.
- The ball must be moved from tire to tire a total of four times. Each attempt must be a different method of transfer than the last.
- If a rule is broken, the ball must be returned to the last successful tire, and the team must start again.
- No one should call others by their last names or use put-downs.

Possible Solutions

This challenge has a multitude of solutions to it, and four are offered in the *Team Building Through Physical Challenges* book. The students can figure out ways to lift the ball by squeezing it with their bodies and moving collectively as a team. Or, they can lay on the ground in two parallel lines (similar to railroad tracks), and as the ball moves along the "human tracks," the team members keep adjusting positions to lengthen the two lines. When the ball gets near a tire, at least four group members should help position the ball onto the tire.

Conclusion of the Challenge

When the team has successfully moved the ball four times, each time a different way, and placed it in a tire without breaking any rules, the challenge is complete.

Additions and Variations

- Put obstacles between the tires for students to go over and duck under.
- Time the challenge and set a course record.
- Lengthen or shorten the distance between tires.

BRIDGE OVER THE RAGING RIVER

Description

Bridge Over the Raging River is a challenge that requires all group members to be integral parts of the solution as they cross a river. The difference between this challenge and Whole World is the students' use of physical assistance. Students must ask or offer physical assistance to one another. They must help one another balance as they walk across an unstable bridge.

Success Criteria

This challenge is mastered when all group members have successfully crossed the river without breaking the rules and have brought all equipment with them.

Equipment

- Automobile tires, 14-inch (4)
- Two-by-fours, 8 feet (2)
- Jump ropes, or clothesline rope, 6-8 feet (2)

Setup

Label distinct starting and ending lines, and use a straight, open area, such as the length of a gym. There should not be any walls close to the route of this challenge. Place all of the equipment behind the starting line. Group members should be behind the starting line, on the "beach."

Remind groups that the two-by-four boards must be moved safely, which includes being careful not to accidentally hit teammates or step on one end so that it flips up.

Rules and Sacrifices

- Group members may not touch the floor.
- A group member may not step on a two-by-four if it has one end in the river.
- If a rule is broken, the group must take all equipment back to the starting position and start over.
- No one should call others by their last names or use put-downs.

Possible Solutions

The group members can make a movable bridge. As the group advances, it passes the tires and the two-by-fours forward.

Group members must share spaces on a tire. Teammates should move slowly, and they should physically assist one another throughout this challenge. The successful team crosses the river with all the equipment in their possession. When group members have concluded their challenge, have them take the equipment back to the starting line for the next group to use.

Conclusion of the Challenge

When all team members and all equipment have successfully crossed the river, the challenge is complete.

Additions and Variations

The best variation we have found is to time the challenge.

KNIGHTS OF THE AROUND TABLE

During the past few years, we have been to many clinics and workshops conducting team-building challenges. Knights of the Around Table has been a favorite challenge of nearly all the workshops. It is a tough challenge, one that forces the team to physically support and encourage one another. This challenge was introduced in the second team-building book, *More Team Building Challenges.*

Description

This challenge produces sore muscles and bruises but also happy smiles and elevated self-confidence. Beginning behind the starting line, the group must figure out how to successfully get everyone to the finish line.

Success Criteria

When all group members have successfully gone from the starting line, over the top of the table, under the table, and again over the top of the table, without touching the floor, and are standing behind the finish line, the challenge has been successful.

Equipment

- Sturdy table, about 3-by-5-feet (1)
- Roll of gym marking tape, or athletic tape (1)
- Large folding mats, 6-by-8-feet or 5-by-10-feet (2)

Setup

Place the mats side by side. Set the table on top of the mats. Make sure that the table is not wobbly and that the table legs are secure. Tape an eight-foot starting line three feet from the side of the table. The finish line should be three feet from the opposite side of the table. See figure 3.2 for a diagram of Knights of the Around Table.

Rules and Sacrifices

- If a group member touches the floor between the starting line and finish line, that person, plus a sacrificed person, must start over. (A sacrificed person is one that has already successfully gotten to the finish line.)

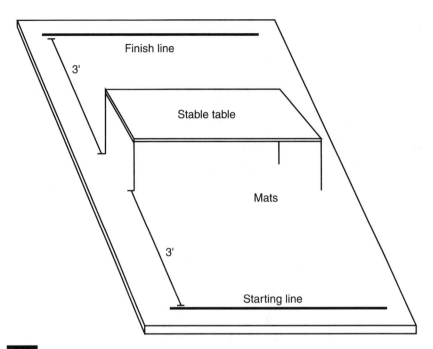

Figure 3.2 Setup for Knights of the Around Table.
Reprinted, by permission, from D.W. Midura and D.R. Glover, 1995, *More team building challenges* (Champaign, IL: Human Kinetics), 48-50.

- Once a group member leaves the table and is standing behind the finish line, he or she may not get back on the table.
- Group members who are standing behind the starting line or finish line may assist the group member who is attempting to go around the table, but they may not touch the table. If the challenge is too difficult for your group, allow two other people (besides the person going around) to touch the table. If a fourth person touches the table, it is a failed attempt. Make sure to watch the table and enforce the rule—it constantly forces kids to communicate with one another.
- Negative pressure and put-downs are not allowed.
- No one may call a teammate by his or her last name.

Possible Solutions

Team success during this challenge is impossible without a strategy to physically assist all team members. Team members should select the most athletic person to go first, and the team should try as best they can to assist that person from behind the starting line. The best way to go around the table is to straddle it from underneath, then roll to the top.

Getting someone to the finish line and allowing them to help from that position is helpful. The team must constantly communicate how they plan to assist one another and how many teammates are currently touching the table. Team members going around the table must verbally communicate to their teammates how the team can best assist them.

Conclusion of the Challenge

The challenge is mastered when all team members are standing behind the finish line after traveling over, under, and then over the table again.

Additions and Variations

- Use a wider table.
- Allow more or fewer team members to touch the table.
- Put a tire under the table for some members to rest on.
- Put a time limit on the journey.

Tell students that when teammates are attempting this challenge to give them some loud encouragement to give them a little extra boost and effort.

New Challenges

The following challenges have come from a team-building graduate class offered through Saint Mary's College of Winona, Minnesota. Teachers in pursuit of their master's degree must produce a team-building challenge as one criterion for credit in this class. The teachers of this class, Dan Midura and Don Glover, have a folder that is full of new team-building challenges. Here are a few from that Saint Mary's class.

JUGGLER'S CARRY

The designers of this challenge were Jeff Lagoo, Kim Peppin, and Tammy Bernard. This challenge is similar to Whole World but requires much more teamwork and support.

Description

The team must transfer four large balls halfway across the gym. Four trips are needed, and each trip requires that the group add one ball. On the first trip, they transport one ball; on the second trip, they add another ball and transport two. This cycle continues until the team completes the fourth trip by transporting four balls.

Success Criteria

This challenge is mastered when all four balls have been picked up one at a time and have crossed from the starting line to the finish line.

Equipment

- Large rubber balls (4) (the size of the ball used depends on the size of your students; we suggest 22 inches or larger) (or light rubber roto-molded balls, beach balls, cage balls)
- Long rope, 20-30 feet (1)
- Chairs (2)

Setup

Place two balls behind the starting line and the finish line, each of which could be placed at the end lines of a basketball court. Place two more balls in the center of the gym behind the half-court line. If no basketball court is available, mark two lines with tape about 30 to 50 feet apart. In the middle of the area, place two chairs with a rope tied between them. The rope should be about the height of the participants' knees. See figure 3.3 for a diagram of Juggler's Carry.

Rules and Sacrifices

- No ball may touch the floor between the starting, half-court, and finish lines.
- Team members may not touch the balls with their hands.
- A different person or a different group of people must pick up a ball and add it each trip.
- Team members may not touch the rope. If they do, they must take that trip over.
- When traveling across the gym, all team members must be connected and touching a ball.
- No last names or put-downs.
- If any of these rules are broken, the team must start over from the line where the last successful trip was completed.

Possible Solutions

Students need to communicate who should pick up the ball and how it should be transported with everyone touching it. During each trip, the students may add a ball to the group support system and move with the balls

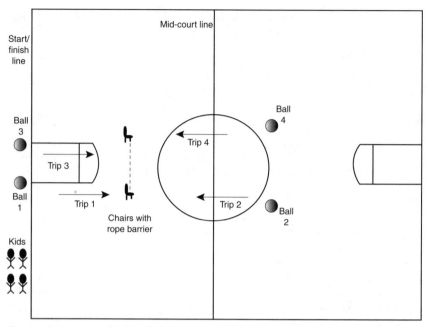

Figure 3.3 Setup for Juggler's Carry.

Reprinted, by permission, from D.R. Glover and D.W. Midura, 1992, *Team building through physical challenges* (Champaign, IL: Human Kinetics), 39-43.

supported by the whole group, or the team may decide to break into smaller groups but still be connected to transport the balls.

Conclusion of the Challenge

The task is complete when all four balls have passed the original starting line.

Additions and Variations

- The team must find a different way to pick up the ball and add it to the group each time.
- The trips can be longer or shorter.
- Two or three of the balls can be smaller (depending on the age of the team).

DYNAMIC BARRIER

This challenge was brought to the program by Jean Skore, David Percival, and Patti Percival. It does not require a lot of equipment, and it can be adapted to students of all ages.

Description

The team must pass through the twirling barrier (rope), from one side to the other without touching the rope. In addition, all equipment must pass through the barrier as well. The twirlers must also pass through the barrier, so the group must decide when to change twirlers.

Success Criteria

This challenge is mastered when all group members and all equipment have passed from one side of the barrier to the other, without touching the barrier.

Equipment

- Long jump rope, 16-foot (1)
- Large ball, 22- to 34-inch (1)
- Deck tennis rings or beanbags (3)
- Hula hoop (1)
- Gym scooter (1)

Setup

Teachers need a large working area so that students are able to twirl the long rope. The twirlers need to practice turning the rope, as this is crucial to the group's success.

Rules and Sacrifices

- All group members and all equipment must pass through the barrier without touching it.
- The large ball must be rolled through and accompanied by a group member. In other words, a team member and the ball must pass through together, but the ball must be rolled.
- The deck tennis rings must be tossed through the barrier and caught by a team member on the opposite side. If a ring is dropped, the challenge must be started over from the beginning.
- The scooter must carry a team member through. The team must decide who sits on the scooter and gets pushed through. *Caution:* Teammates may assist by pushing the scooter and their teammate through, but make sure they are aware of their proximity to the walls. As soon as the scooter gets through, the student should stop it to avoid coasting into other students or equipment.
- Two teammates must pass through at the same time while holding the hula hoop.

- All remaining students on the team must pass through the barrier together. They do not have to be connected, but they do have to pass through at the same time.
- If any teammate or any equipment touches the barrier, then that person or piece of equipment—and all team members who have already successfully passed through the barrier—must go back.
- No last names or put-downs.

Possible Solutions

The rules seem to indicate how this challenge must be solved. The team must decide which team members will pass through the barrier with equipment and which team members will pass through the barrier with other teammates. The team must also decide who will throw and catch the deck tennis rings, who will be the starting twirlers, and who will be replacing them when it is their turn to pass through the barrier.

Additions and Variations

- Don't make equipment the challenging factor—time the team instead. See how long it takes them to pass through the barrier one at a time. This includes switching twirlers. The clock stops only when all teammates have passed through.
- Try having the team pass through the barrier and back while being connected. Have them select their best twirlers because they will not have to pass through in this variation.
- Let the team figure out a new method of passing through the barrier using all the equipment.

FLING IT

Another challenge from the Saint Mary's University program, this one requires minimal equipment. The students must communicate before attempting this challenge, or it could be very difficult to master. This challenge is similar to Whole World and Juggler's Carry except that it uses ropes to transport the ball.

Description

The team must work together to transfer a large ball from the starting line, around a cone about 50 feet away, and back to the starting line.

Success Criteria

Using only ropes, all group members must transfer the ball from the starting point, around the midpoint, back to the starting point. When the ball reaches the base (the "fling-it" point) about 15 feet from the ending point, they must fling it the rest of the way. The ball must be caught behind the line, by two teammates.

Equipment

- Large rubber ball, 22-inch or larger (1)
- Ropes (8)
- Base, or marker (to signify the fling-it spot) (1)

Setup

You will need approximately one-half of a basketball court for this activity. Mark a starting line or use the end line of the basketball court. Place a cone about 40 to 50 feet away, or place it at the center line of the court. Place the base 15 feet from the starting line. Put the ball behind the starting line, resting on the floor. See figure 3.4 for a diagram of Fling It.

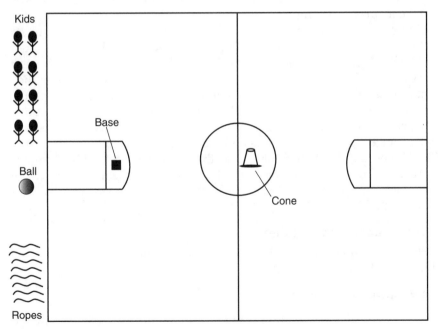

Figure 3.4 Setup of Fling It.

Rules and Sacrifices

- The ball must never touch the floor between the starting line and the finish line.
- Teammates must not touch the ball with their hands or bodies after crossing the starting line and beginning the transport.
- Once the ball reaches the base on the return trip, it must be flung by using the ropes as flingers. The ball must be caught by two team members behind the starting line. The catchers, designated by their team, may use their hands to catch the ball, but they must stay behind the starting line.
- The ball must be caught in the air by the catchers.
- No last names or put-downs.
- If any rule is broken, the team must return to the starting line and begin the challenge again.

Possible Solutions

The team has to discuss how to arrange the ropes to best carry and transport the ball. They may lay them straight and side-by-side, or criss-cross them to form a carrying pouch.

Designated team members may place the ball in the desired position on the ropes and use their hands to do it. Remember that the hands cannot touch the ball after it crosses the starting line, but they may be used behind the starting line. The team has to pick up the ball on signal, and once they have it stabilized, they may start their journey. After they go around the midpoint line and are headed back to the starting line, they must stop at the base and prepare to fling the ball to the starting line. Two members of the team must drop their ropes and place themselves behind the starting line. These are the catchers. On signal, the teammates left holding the ropes must fling the ball to the catchers, who must catch it behind the line. The toss or fling must be done in a controlled, rhythmic manner, or the ball will not reach the catchers.

Conclusion of the Challenge

Fling It is completed when the group has successfully tossed the ball to the catchers and when the catchers catch the ball in the air.

Additions and Variations

- This challenge could become much more difficult by increasing the size or weight of the ball.

- To add excitement, place a rope to step over or duck under as the group transports the ball.
- Place the base farther away from the ball to make this challenge much more difficult.
- Time the challenge, and encourage your students to set class records.

FRANKENSTEIN

This challenge is a beat-the-clock challenge. The kids will love it. This challenge also reinforces the human anatomy lesson the science teacher is working on.

Description

The students attempt to put together the skeleton puzzle in the fastest time possible. The team has to earn the right to put Frankenstein together by successfully tossing and catching a deck tennis ring. Each time the ring has been successfully passed, the team gets to add three more bones to Frankenstein. Seven trips of tossing the ring are required to build Frankenstein.

Success Criteria

Frankenstein is mastered when students put all of his bones in the correct place.

Equipment

- Skeleton puzzle (1)
- Deck tennis ring (1)
- Storage crate (1)
- Indoor bases (5)

Setup

Place the bases about 10 to 15 feet apart in a straight line in your gym. The distance depends on the age and ability level of your students. Instruct five of the team members to one base each. The remaining team members must be in the Frankenstein-building area, close to base 1. The storage crate holding the skeleton puzzle should be at the opposite end of the gym, or about 15 feet from base 5. See figure 3.5 for a diagram of Frankenstein.

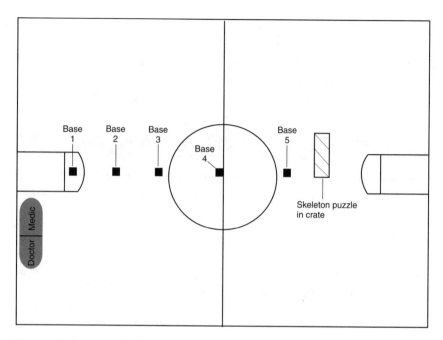

Figure 3.5 Setup for Frankenstein.

Rules and Sacrifices

- The deck tennis ring must be successfully tossed from base 1 to base 2. The person on base 2 must catch the ring and successfully turn and toss it to the person on base 3. This process continues until the ring has traveled all the way to base 5 and back to base 1. If the ring is dropped, it must be sent back to the teammate that last tossed the ring.

- Once the ring gets back to base 1, the medic must run to the storage crate at the opposite end of the gym and bring back three bones. The medic cannot leave the Frankenstein-building area until the ring gets back to base 1.

- When the medic returns, he or she must give the bones to the doctors, who must start assembling the puzzle. When the doctors get the bones, all players need to rotate positions. The medic goes to base 1; base 1 goes to base 2; and so on. Base 5 becomes a new doctor, and one of the doctors becomes the new medic. Players cannot rotate positions until the medic returns to the Frankenstein-building area with three bones and the doctors place the bones in the correct positions and yell, "Done."

- The ring needs to make seven successful round-trips to get all puzzle pieces to the Frankenstein-building area. After the last medic has delivered the last three puzzle pieces, the team hustles to the lab and confers whether any changes need to be made to Frankenstein to make him correct. When they think Frankenstein has been put together correctly, the last medic yells, "Lightning!" This is the signal to stop the clock. The teacher then checks the puzzle for accuracy. If it is correct, the time stands. If it is incorrect, the clock starts again as the team rearranges the bones. This process continues until Frankenstein is correct.

Possible Solutions

Before the challenge starts, the team should communicate where certain teammates should position themselves. Certainly, students want the best catchers on the bases, and the teammate who would make a good doctor should plan to rotate to the puzzle when most of the bones are there.

Conclusion of the Challenge

When Frankenstein is assembled correctly, the clock stops and the challenge is complete.

Additions and Variations

- Allow teammates to assign permanent roles so that they can match the team members' skills with the challenge.
- Lengthen or shorten the distance of the toss.
- Bring back more or fewer bones to lengthen or shorten the time of the challenge.

THE MAZE

This challenge has been around for a while. We have used it at workshops and team-bulding classes for quite a few years. While not a physical challenge, the team must pay attention to what other teammates do and say. Variations on this challenge are especially fun.

Description

The team must take turns stepping onto bases to complete a predetermined path. The first team member steps on a poly spot designated as the start by the leader. The leader holds a key to the correct path through the poly spots and gives a yes-or-no response for a correct or incorrect step by a team member (figure 3.6). The teammate attempting to negotiate the maze may continue stepping as long as yes-responses are received from the leader. As soon as a no-response is received, the teammate must leave the maze and rejoin the team. The next member of the group attempts to complete the maze by going as far as the preceding teammate and trying to add on to the path. The team tries to get all members through the maze without any errors.

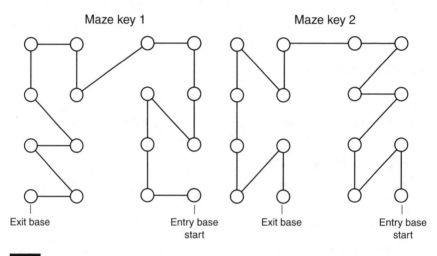

Figure 3.6 Teachers can make up their own keys to The Maze when these become familiar to students.

Success Criteria

The maze will be mastered when all group members have successfully traveled from the starting point, through the maze, and out the designated ending point.

Equipment

- Poly spots, 12-inch (16)
- Maze key cards (see the appendix for two sample cards)

Setup

Place all 16 poly spots on the floor, 4 across by 4 down. Give the leader the key, and instruct the leader to keep the key hidden from the rest of the team.

Rules and Sacrifices

- Team members may only continue when they make a correct step.
- The entire group must start over on a miss, regardless of how many members have successfully completed the maze.
- Group members may only step on a base when it is their turn.
- Each base may be used only once.
- Group members may not use last names or put-downs.

Possible Solutions

Group members must pay close attention to the success and failures of preceding group members. They need to rely on one another for correct steps through the maze, especially if they have forgotten what is a *yes* and what is a *no*. A quick group discussion and agreement might be warranted before someone takes their turn.

Conclusion of the Challenge

When all group members have succeeded in negotiating the maze without a miss, the challenge will be mastered.

Additions and Variations

- Increase or decrease the amount of bases according to the age level of the team.
- Make up new maze patterns.
- Do not allow any type of communication (verbal and nonverbal), or allow only nonverbal communication.
- Blindfold one member of the group after figuring out the solution. The team must then attempt to help the blind person get through the maze by verbal communication only. Caution the blind teammate not to move unless instructed to do so by teammates. Make sure the area is clear.

TOXIC SPLASH

This is another Saint Mary's Challenge created by Henry Gerten, Julie Nasuik, and Dawn Woelfel. This challenge requires a lot of equipment, but all of it is probably in your gym storeroom.

Description

In this challenge, the students are encouraged to clean up the river of pollutants and toxins, which are killing the fish. During the clean-up, the raft, which is holding the team and the six buckets of collected hazardous materials, suddenly begins to sink. To save the team and the river from contamination, students must get the toxic materials to land and safely dispose of them before the raft sinks.

Success Criteria

All the team members and all the toxic materials must make it across the river, and they must finish in the designated area.

Equipment

- Small panel mats (3)
- Low balance beam (1)
- Small tire (1)
- Long poles, 5 to 7 feet (2)
- Plastic ice cream buckets (6)
- Items to fill the bucket (packing peanuts, golf balls, tennis balls, beanbags)
- Mats (to place around the beam for safety)

Setup

Place a mat on the floor (the raft)—this is the starting position for team members. Place the low balance beam (the log) three feet in front of the mat. At the other end of the beam, place another mat (the sand bar) three feet from the end of the beam. Place a tire (the rock) three feet from the sand bar. After the rock, place another mat (land) three feet away. See figure 3.7 for a diagram of Toxic Splash.

Rules and Sacrifices

- If a bucket touches any part of a team member's body, then that team member—plus a successful team member—must return to the raft with their buckets of toxic materials.
- If any team member or any pole touches the river, the team member who made the error, plus one successful team member, must return to the raft with their bucket.
- If any toxic material spills out of the bucket into the river or onto the land, the guilty team member who commits the error, plus an innocent bystander (another teammate), must be sacrificed.
- Only one person can be holding a pole at any time.
- The pole on the log and rock may not leave those places. They should remain on the log and rock after all toxic materials have been moved.

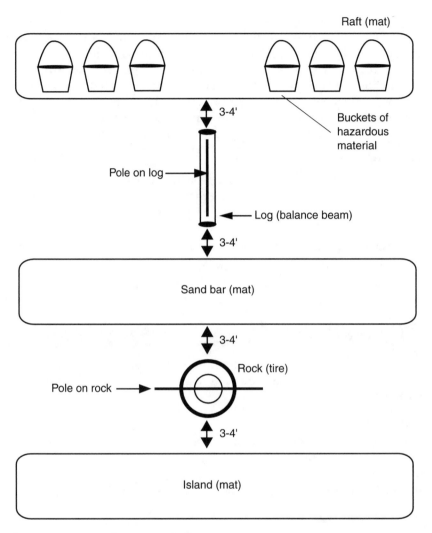

Figure 3.7 Setup for Toxic Splash.

- Students should not use last names or put-downs.
- Any violation of any rule results in a one-plus-one sacrifice (the team-mate who erred plus one other).

Possible Solutions

Students must move slowly, and they must help one another balance when-ever possible. One student should move forward to the rock and pick up the pole; another student should position herself on the log. The students must try to pick up the toxic waste with the poles. They must transfer the waste all the way to the land, using only the poles. The two students who transported the first two buckets now must help each other to land, and two more students should come forward to transport the next two buckets, as chosen by the group. The team may want to match the skill levels of each team member to the weight of each bucket (some are heavier than others). This sequence continues until all buckets are transported to land. The students should move slowly and encourage one another.

Conclusion of the Challenge

When all the toxic-waste buckets and team members are on land and when the poles are balanced on the log and rock, the challenge is complete.

Additions and Variations

- Set a time limit—everyone has to be off the raft before it sinks.
- Make buckets heavier and lighter.
- Allow younger children to touch poles simultaneously.

MAGIC BASES

This challenge was given to us by Jimmy Gehm, a physical educator in Missouri. Jimmy was kind enough to share his favorite team builder with us and allow us to use it.

Description

The team must hold hands and travel through a set of 12-inch poly spots, laid in a figure-eight pattern. The team cannot speak nor can they touch the floor. During this journey, the group will have to communicate, but they will have to do so in some manner other than talking.

Success Criteria

Magic Bases is completed when all group members successfully complete the figure-eight pattern and exit the last base.

Equipment

- Poly spots (one for each member of the team making the journey, plus one extra)

Setup

Set up the poly spots in a figure-eight pattern. The distance between the spots should not exceed two feet. The age and size of your students should dictate the distance between spots; that is, younger children will need to have them closer. Spots should be placed no farther than a big step away. One base should be the entrance base, and one base should be the exit base. See figure 3.8 for a diagram of Magic Bases.

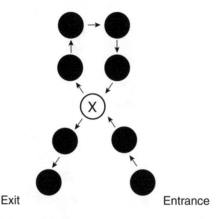

Exit   Entrance

Figure 3.8 Setup of Magic Bases.

Rules and Sacrifices

- The team must travel the figure-eight route while holding hands. If they disconnect hands at any time, the whole group must start over.
- No more than two feet on a poly spot at one time.
- Team members may not touch the floor.
- No last names or put-downs.
- If any rule is broken, the group must start over.

Possible Solutions

The team must take it slow and help one another balance on the bases. When students hop or step to a new base, the person they are connected to could be pulled off a base. When the team meets at the crossroad of the figure-eight pattern, they have to nonverbally communicate as to how they will cross. One group either holds their arms low so that the lead group can step over, or they hold their arms high so that the rest of the group can pass under. The team has to take turns passing over or under the arms of their teammates at the intersection of the figure eight.

Conclusion of the Challenge

This challenge is mastered when all team members have successfully traveled the figure-eight pattern of bases without touching the floor or becoming disconnected.

Additions and Variations

- Designate one base as the speaking base. Students may not talk until they reach that base. This allows each student some input during the challenge.
- Time the challenge.
- Once the first person in line reaches the fifth base, the team must figure out how to make that person either last off the course or last in line.
- Allow more than two feet on any base at one time.

RAIDERS OF THE LOST JEWEL

This challenge comes from Travis Olson and Andy Viker, who were classmates in the team-building class run by Saint Mary's University. Many students attend this class during the summer, and as part of a final project, the students must develop a challenge and present it to the class. I think this challenge is one of the best I have seen during the last five years of reviewing student challenges. It does not require a lot of equipment or space, and it involves the whole team, both mentally and physically.

Description

The team must figure out how to get the lost jewel out of the jungle and back to its rightful place in the museum. They must remove the jewel from its resting place and get it to the museum, which is outside of the center circle on a basketball court.

Success Criteria

The team achieves success when the ball (the jewel) has completed three successful trips to the outside of the center circle.

Equipment

- Large cone, 12-24 inches (1)
- Dowels, wood or metal, or track batons about 18-24 inches (2)
- Cloth ropes (4) (the length of which should be slightly shorter than the center circle diameter)

- Center circle on a basketball court, or make a large circle out of rope (about 10 feet in diameter)

Setup

Place the cone in the center of the circle, with the ball balanced on top. The team members and all other pieces of equipment should be on the outside of the circle.

Rules and Sacrifices

- No group member may step inside the circle at any point during the challenge.
- The ball may not touch the ground inside or outside the circle.
- The ball must be successfully removed from the circle three different times. Each time, it must be removed a different way.
- No one can use last names or put-downs.
- If any rule is broken, the ball must return to the starting point and the effort must be repeated.
- Do not allow students to tie the rope to a dowel and attempt to swing the rope and "tap" the ball off of the cone.

Possible Solutions

The team must come up with three solutions. Here are three we have found:

- To create a modified net, students can cross the four ropes at the center of the circle. They can then attempt to walk the ball to the outside.
- Same as above, except that the team could instead attempt to fling the ball and catch it outside the circle.
- The ropes could be tied to the end of the dowels, and the dowels could be used to capture the ball. The dowels would have to pass over the top of the ball, then rest on the floor. As students start pulling the dowels up the cone, they could pick the ball off the top.

Conclusion of the Challenge

When the ball has been successfully transported to the outside of the circle three different ways, the challenge is mastered.

Additions and Variations

- Use a heavier ball.
- Make the circle larger.
- Make the ropes a little shorter.
- Time the challenge.

FACTOR IN

This is another challenge created by teachers in the team-building program offered through Saint Mary's University. This challenge was created by Marc Bachman and Jay Ehlers. The unique thing about this challenge is that it incorporates math and puzzle skills into a great team-building challenge.

Description

The team must remain connected and move through a maze of numbered bases. The team members must stand on various bases in the maze, but the bases they are using must have a total number that can be factored by three.

Success Criteria

The task is mastered when all group members move from one side of the maze to the other while connected, keeping the sum total of the bases being used a factor of three.

Equipment

- Round bases, with numbers written or taped on top (12)

Setup

The bases should be set on the floor in the following pattern:

12	11	10
7	8	9
6	5	4
1	2	3

Rules and Sacrifices

- Team members must stay connected during travel.
- Team members may only move one base at a time.
- Team members may move in a straight or diagonal path.
- Teammates must remain one base away from the immediate person they are connected to.
- Only one team member may enter the maze at a time. When a teammate gets to the last row of the maze, that teammate may step out of the maze but must stay connected with the others.
- After each team member enters or exits the maze, the total-sum number (of the bases team members are standing on) must be a factor of three. Otherwise, the team must start again.

- Only one person on a base at a time.
- No one should call others by last names or use put-downs.

Possible Solutions

As each team member enters or exits the maze, the team needs to add up the numbers they are standing on. If the numbers add up to a factor of three, the team can continue.

Conclusion of the Challenge

When the whole team has successfully moved through the maze and is standing together at the finish, the challenge is complete.

Additions and Variations

- To make the challenge easier, only use numerals 1, 2, and 3.
- To make the challenge more difficult, randomly place the bases. One factor of three should be in each row.
- Time the challenge.
- Add more rows.

RAINBOW SWAMP TRAIL

This challenge uses minimal equipment but requires that the group use constant communication and physical support while attempting to solve it.

Description

Each member of the team must get to the other side of the swamp, and along the way, they each must retrieve a beanbag and take it with them to the shore. Stepping stones are in the swamp so that the group can plan a route. The stepping stones are slippery and can only hold one teammate at a time. Be careful and don't fall into the swamp!

Success Criteria

When all of the team members and beanbags make it to the opposite shore successfully, the team has mastered the challenge.

Equipment

- Poly spot markers, 12-inch (12)
- Rainbow beanbags (1 for each team member)

Setup

Designate a starting line and finish line, about 15 feet apart (the swamp lies between these two lines). Place the poly spots (the stepping stones) in two straight lines between the two lines. The poly spots should be about one giant step apart. This spacing will vary upon the age of your students—up to three feet for middle school and down to 18 inches for first graders. Place the six beanbags at poly spots numbers 2, 3, 6, 7, 9, and 10. The beanbags should vary in distance away from the poly spot. They should range from two feet to four feet away. Again, this spacing depends upon the age and size of your students. A five-foot person can get a beanbag four feet away without stepping off the spot . . . but needs a lot of support to reach it. Here is a suggested list of distances for a group of sixth graders.

- The yellow beanbag—3 feet away from poly spot number 2
- The red beanbag—2 feet away from poly spot number 3
- The green beanbag—4 feet away from poly spot number 5
- The orange beanbag—3 1/2 feet away from poly spot number 7
- The blue beanbag—2 feet away from poly spot number 9
- The purple beanbag—4 feet away from poly spot number 10

See figure 3.9 for a diagram of Rainbow Swamp Trail.

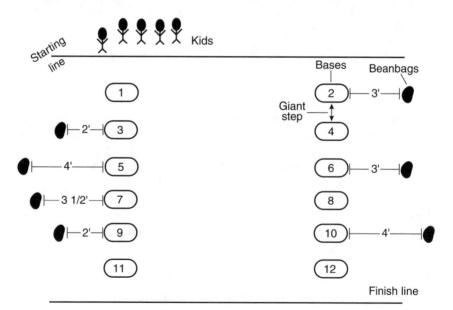

Figure 3.9 Setup for Rainbow Swamp Trail.

Rules and Sacrifices

- The team must hold hands and stay connected throughout their trip through the swamp. When a teammate attempts to pick up a bean-bag, students may disconnect hands, but they must reconnect before continuing the journey.
- No one may touch the floor during the trip through the swamp. If either this rule or the previous rule is broken, the group must start over.
- Each team member must collect one beanbag on their journey and take it across the swamp.
- Students should not use last names or put-downs during the challenge.

Possible Solutions

The team has to discuss which team member should get which beanbag. The taller teammates have to get the beanbags that are the farthest away. The team also has to figure out how to best assist the students who cannot reach their beanbags easily. The team must move slowly and be in constant communication or risk pulling a teammate off a stepping stone.

Conclusion of the Challenge

The challenge is over when all team members and beanbags are on the shore behind the finish line.

Additions and Variations

- Make one base a slippery base. The rule for this base is that only one foot is allowed to touch this base at one time.
- Make the team silent, except for one person who must direct the team.
- Time the team and set a course record.

GEO SPHERE

This challenge is from Tom Heck, who is known internationally as the "Teach Me Teamwork Coach" (**www.tomheck.com**). Tom specializes in helping educators—especially classroom teachers—teach leadership and team skills to students, with amazing results such as increased test scores and improved control of the classroom. Tom's books, videos, audiotape programs, Web sites, workshops, and team-building games utilize the most effective aspects of adventure-based, experiential education. Tom has worked with educators from around the world, and his success stems from his experience as a public school teacher, juvenile corrections officer, and as a senior director in the largest nonprofit youth serving agency in the country. Tom designed the Geo Sphere challenge and shared it with us for this book.

Description

The team must set up a geo sphere so that it is balanced and upright in the bucket. The team must then plan travel routes through the geo sphere without causing it to collapse. This is a tough challenge when students use its variations (listed in the Additions and Variations section).

Success Criteria

This challenge is mastered when all team members have passed through the geo sphere without causing it to tumble.

Equipment

- Geo sphere (1)
- Multipurpose bucket (1)

Setup

Place the collapsed geo sphere and the bucket on the floor. The team can gather nearby and start discussion as to how to set up the geo sphere. Once it's set up, they may continue solving the challenge.

Rules and Sacrifices

- The team members must travel through the geo sphere one at a time (figure 3.10). When one team member has used a pathway or entrance-to-exit route, that unique sequence of travel cannot be used by another team member. The same openings can be used but not in the same sequence.
- If a team member bumps the geo sphere, causing it to collapse, the entire team must start over from the beginning.
- Teammates may communicate and physically assist other teammates as they attempt to pass through.
- No one may stabilize the geo sphere to prevent its tipping over.
- No one may dive through the geo sphere.
- No last names or put-downs.

Possible Solutions

The team should discuss travel plans first. They need to be clear about other teammates' routes so that no route is inadvertently repeated. Team-

Figure 3.10 Team members travel through the geo sphere.
© Gopher Sport/Kim Poliszuk

mates should be talking to the person traveling through the geo sphere, letting them know how close they are to touching the geo sphere. Team members should move slowly and cautiously.

Conclusion of the Challenge

When everyone has passed through the geo sphere and it is still standing, the challenge has been mastered. Now, try it again with some additions and variations.

Additions and Variations

- Challenge the group to form a line, holding hands, then travel through. Make the group travel through at least three different pathways without dropping hands.
- Suspend a string with a ball from the top of the geo sphere so that it hangs through the center of the geo sphere. This will act as a barrier and will increase the level of difficulty. No one should be allowed to touch the ball.
- Time the travel, and set class records.

- In pairs, ask the students to coach their partner through. The partner doing the traveling must wear a blindfold or keep their eyes closed.
- Pass a large object through the upper half of the geo sphere, such as a football dummy or a box of some kind.
- Adjust the string on the geo sphere to make it wider or narrower.

INTEGRITY TOWER

This is a brand new challenge that further connects character education and team building. The students must work together to build a tower of bricks, which are made of foam and labeled *Character, Respect, Sportspersonship, Judgment, Pride,* and *Integrity.* This challenge is difficult for elementary school children to master, but it could be quite easy for middle school.

Description

The students must transport the foam blocks with a partner and build a tower at the designated site 20 feet away. The blocks should be spread out on the floor, with the team huddled around them. The team must figure out how to transport the blocks to the building site. Once they get a block to the building site, they must figure out how they will work together to build the tower.

Success Criteria

The team is successful when the blocks are stacked in the type of tower the teacher requested.

Equipment

- Foam blocks (6)

Setup

Mark the blocks *Character, Respect, Sportspersonship, Judgment, Pride,* and *Integrity.* Place the bricks on the floor. Designate a building site about 20 to 30 feet away. The students must figure out how to transport the blocks to the building site. Once they get a block to the site, they must figure out how they will work together to build the tower.

Rules and Sacrifices

- Each block must be transported by two teammates, and each pair of partners may transport only one block at a time.

- The blocks may never be touched by anyone's hands nor can the blocks ever touch the ground—except for the *Character* block, which must be the first block transported. All other blocks are built upon the *Character* block.

- Each block must be transported using a different combination of body parts. No two partners can transport a block in the same method of another pair of teammates. For example, the first set of partners may use their elbows; the second set of partners may use their knees; and so on.

- Teammates may not help partners during the transport phase of the challenge, but they may help teammates stack the blocks on the tower—as long as they don't use their hands. The teammates that transported the block must still be the principal stackers. They cannot relinquish control of the block, but other teammates may assist by steadying the tower or balancing a block while it is being placed.

- The *Integrity* block is the last block to be placed.

- No put-downs or last names allowed.

- If any of these rules are broken, the group must take all blocks to the starting point and start over.

Possible Solutions

The team has to decide first who works together. Each pair then discusses among themselves how to transport their block so that the method used is unique to their team.

When teammates decide the method of moving the blocks to the building site, the team needs to help one another stack the blocks. Teammates who are finished transporting should assist teammates who are attempting to stack a block.

Conclusion of the Challenge

When the tower is complete and stable within the building site, the challenge is mastered.

Additions and Variations

- Make the students go over and under an obstacle while transporting their blocks.

- Design different towers.

- Make sure all character-education words are facing the same direction.

TWIST-AND-TURN MARBLE CHALLENGE

This challenge should be a New Year's Eve party game. Our college elementary education students really loved this one, and we think it will become a favorite of yours as well. This challenge is adaptable for all ages, and it can be adapted to be very easy or very difficult.

Description

Students try to pass three marbles from one end of a tube to the other. The teammates must watch the marbles and communicate to others where the marbles are at all times. Teammates can also physically assist each other.

Success Criteria

When all three marbles have been passed through the entire length of the tube, the challenge is complete.

Equipment

- Twist-and-turn marble race track (1)
- Marbles (3)

Setup

Arrange a team of six students in a long, straight line along the length of the tube, which should be lying on the floor, stretched out to its full length. Each student attaches a waist belt first, then a left-arm strap and a right-arm strap, so that all six teammates are connected to the tube by their three straps. Make sure the distance between all waist belts is equal with about two feet of tube between each student.

The first team member in line puts one marble into the tube and attempts to pass it to the second team member. Once the second team member has successfully passed the marble to the third team member, the first team member should start the second marble. This sequence continues until all three marbles have been passed and received, and the marbles come out the other end of the tube.

Rules and Sacrifices

- Team members may not touch the tube with their hands.
- The team must pass three marbles through the entire length of the tube without ever letting the marbles touch.
- Students cannot use put-downs or last names.
- The first student in line may momentarily hold the tube to insert the marble.

- Teammates may physically assist one another.
- If any rule is broken, all three marbles must be returned to the first teammate, and the challenge starts over.

Possible Solutions

The way the challenge is described, the students must vary the height of their arms to keep the marble moving. One teammate may have to get lower to receive the marble, then stand tall once they have possession of the marble. The marble is not easy to see. All teammates must help one another by spotting the marble and communicating. Also, when a marble gets stuck, team members may either move the tube with their feet or touch the tube with other parts of their body—just not their hands. Team members may physically assist one another as well as verbally communicate instructions.

Conclusion of the Challenge

When all three marbles have passed through the tube and have not touched one another, the challenge is complete.

Additions and Variations

- By connecting at the waist and both arms, the students are attempting the easiest variation. Try using your imagination and connect other parts of the body to the tube. For example, arm-waist-knee or knee-waist-knee. Or, if you would like to make it more difficult, go completely around the waist.
- Time the challenge.

COCONUT COLLECTION

With all the neat gym scooter accessories on the market today, we decided to create an activity using the river raft and river raft paddles. If you don't have a river raft, try putting a mat on top of three scooters.

Description

The team must paddle the rafts across the river, stopping at each of the islands to pick up coconuts. They must then deliver the coconuts to the opposite shore. This challenge calls for a lot of communication and teamwork. If your class has teams with eight teammates, then two rafts can carry three team members and one raft could carry two. If the students are small, they could also fit four on two rafts.

Success Criteria

When the team has delivered all 24 coconuts to the shore, the challenge is mastered.

Equipment

- River rafts (3)
- Gym scooters, 16-inch (6)
- Scooter paddles (6)
- Hula hoops (6)
- Balloons, 9-inch diameter (24)

Setup

Select a starting line and a finish line. The distance should be approximately one-half the length of the gym. The area between the starting line and finish line is the river. Lay the six hula hoops (the islands) in zigzag fashion about 15 feet apart, between the starting line and finish line. Equally distribute the balloons (the coconuts) in each hoop. The challenge is to see how many coconuts a team can successfully transfer (without dropping) to the opposite shore.

Rules and Sacrifices

- If a team member touches the floor, all river rafts must return to the starting line.
- If a balloon touches the floor, all river rafts must be returned to the starting line and all coconuts returned to the islands.
- All equipment (coconuts, paddles, and rafts) must make it to shore.
- No put-downs or last names.

Possible Solutions

The team must figure out how many balloons are able to fit on a raft. It isn't easy paddling a raft and trying to carry a balloon. The team has to decide who paddles the rafts and who gathers and carries the coconuts. Perhaps the rafts can form a large barge so that balloons can be wedged between teammates. The rules do not say that all balloons must be brought over in one attempt, so two trips for some rafters may be necessary.

Conclusion of the Challenge

When all balloons, team members, rafts, and paddles are on shore, the challenge is mastered.

Additions and Variation

- Add obstacles in the river to encourage more paddling.
- Let the rafts race, or set a time limit for the entire team.
- Link the three rafts together.
- Vary the size of the team or length of the river.
- Use fewer paddles.

Note: The team may not be able to get all the balloons to the opposite shore. You may have to reduce the number of balloons for younger students.

THE GREAT PEARL CAPER

This challenge requires special equipment. It is quite difficult for primary school levels but perfect for intermediate and middle school levels. The team must successfully transport the giant pearl back to its rightful place. This challenge can be much more difficult with some of the clever variations mentioned at the end of the challenge.

Description

The team has two pearl track transports. They must work together to transport the pearl across the gym and figure out how to place it in its pearl stand (a tire). They must remember that they cannot move forward when the ball is in their pearl track transport.

Success Criteria

When the pearl is in its pearl stand, the challenge is mastered.

Equipment

- Pearl track transports (2)
- Ball, 22-inch or larger (1)
- Tires, 15-inch (2)

Setup

Place the cage ball (the pearl) on the tire behind the starting line. The finish line is located at the midcourt line of the gym. The tire (the pearl stand) is located on the finish line. When the pearl is successfully deposited in the stand, the challenge is complete (figure 3.11). The team members and the pearl track transports are all located at the starting line with the pearl.

Figure 3.11 Setup for The Great Pearl Caper. Here a crate is used as the pearl stand instead of a tire.
© Gopher Sport/Kim Poliszuk

Rules and Sacrifices

- The pearl cannot be touched by any part of any team member's body.
- The pearl can only be transported by the pearl track transports.
- Once a team has the pearl in their track transport, that team cannot move toward the pearl stand. They can move anywhere if they are not in possession of the pearl.
- The pearl may never touch the ground.
- No put-downs or last names allowed.
- If any rule is broken, the team must return to the starting line, replace the pearl on the tire, and attempt the challenge again.

Possible Solutions

One pearl-track-transport team has to push the pearl off the first tire and onto the other team's pearl track transport. The receiving pearl-track-transport team must receive the ball off the ground, and they must balance it until the other team can move into place to receive the ball.

The teams continue to pass the ball to each other as they make progress toward the second tire. If they move too fast, the ball may drop to the floor. They must carefully roll it down their track and onto the other teammates' waiting track. Once the pearl arrives at the second tire, the team must attempt to carefully roll the ball onto the tire. The other part of the team can attempt to steady it with their transport track. This challenge works best when the students pull the ropes tight to widen the track.

Conclusion of the Challenge

When the ball is resting on the second tire, the challenge is mastered.

Additions and Variations

- Do not allow the students to balance the ball on the transport using the rope handles. Make them pull the ropes tight.
- As they move toward the pearl stand, make the team step over mats or under a high-jump bar.
- Time them, and encourage them to try to set a class record.

TEAM STOMP IT

This is an advanced challenge. It is very difficult, but it can be made easier through the variations discussed at the end of this challenge. This challenge is suitable only for grades 6 through 12.

Description

This challenge can be done with teams of four, five, or six teammates—all of whom are standing on designated poly spots. Five balls are placed on a team stomp-it board. On signal, one teammate launches the balls into the air. All balls must be successfully caught, but each ball must be caught by a different teammate. If this is accomplished, the team may move to the second stage of the challenge. Stomp one ball at a time, which is then batted by the stomper. The stomper repeats this process of batting and stomping four times. Two of the four balls that were batted must be caught by teammates.

Success Criteria

When all five balls are caught by the correct teammates, the first half of the challenge is mastered. The second half of the challenge is complete when two balls are stomped, batted, and successfully caught.

Equipment

- Five-hole stomp-it board (1)
- Stomp-it balls (5)
- Table-tennis paddle (1)
- Poly spots (5)

Setup

The stomp-it board should be placed on a mat. The balls should be placed on the stomp-it board, with the poly spots around the board.

Rules and Sacrifices

- Each team member, including the stomper, must catch one ball. If any ball is dropped, the team must replace the balls and try again. If there are six team members, then the stomper is not required to catch a ball.
- Team members may not leave their poly spots until the stomper hits the stomp-it board.
- Everyone must rotate positions after each failed attempt.
- When all five balls are caught, the team can then select a stomper/ batter. The rest of the team must move their poly spots approximately 20 feet away from the side of the stomp-it board.
- Only one ball at a time can be used for batting.

Possible Solutions

This is a challenge that requires much trial and error. After the first trial, the stomper must communicate to the next stomper how hard to strike the board. In addition, all team members must communicate to one another as to the flight path of their ball.

The team has to select the best possible batter to complete the challenge. The batter must stomp and hit the ball so that one of the five teammates on the bases can catch it. Teammates can decide the best place to put their poly spots to catch the ball.

Conclusion of the Challenge

Conclusion of the first part of this challenge is when all five balls are caught. The second part of the challenge is mastered when two of the four batted balls are caught.

Additions and Variations

- To make this challenge a bit easier, let the kids stay on one base, instead of rotating after each attempt.

- When batting and catching, move the bases closer or farther away, depending upon the age of your students.
- Time the challenge—students love to try and set records
- Allow a larger team to attempt this challenge. A team of 7 or 8 makes it much more difficult.

CHARACTER CUP STACK

This is a brand new team builder that is great fun. It combines good team communication skills and good team planning. This challenge is also an interdisciplinary challenge, mixing Spanish with team building.

Description

The objective of this challenge is to build various pyramids using the buckets. For the description of this challenge, we will assume that the students are in a group of eight. Six of the students are builders, and two students (designated by the group) are the construction managers. The construction managers need the construction keys. The managers must also stay in the construction office, which could be a hoop or mat. When the six construction builders are ready, the construction managers attempt to instruct the builders in building a bucket tower.

Success Criteria

When the bucket tower has been built correctly and is approved by the teacher, the challenge is mastered.

Equipment

- Buckets for stacking (12)
- The Spanish translation of the character-education words:

English	Spanish	English	Spanish
Respect	Respeto	Loyalty	Lealtad
Honesty	Honestidad	Courtesy	Cortecía
Tolerance	Tolerancía	To be an example	Ser un ejemplo
Courage	Corage	Character	Caracter
Enthusiasm	Entusiasmo	Caring	Protección
Pride	Orgullo	Integrity	Integridad

- Stacking keys (3)

Description

The buckets are used to stack one on top of another to build the pyramids. These buckets can be the five-gallon buckets that you can get from your school's food service (e.g., pickles come shipped in five-gallon buckets). The teacher writes a character-education word on one side of each bucket with the Spanish translation written on the other side. The teacher also writes a number (1 through 12) on each bucket.

Setup

Stack the buckets in two columns of six in a starting area, and designate a finish area about 20 feet away, which is where the pyramids will be built. The builders start by the two columns of buckets, and the construction managers start in the finish area (in the construction office). See figure 3.12 for a diagram of Character Cup Stack.

Stacks of buckets (each 6" high)   Building area

⟶

20'

Starting area

Mat for construction managers (construction office)

Figure 3.12   Setup for Character Cup Stack.

Rules and Sacrifices:

- Construction managers may not touch construction builders or buckets.
- Construction managers must stay in the construction office.

- Construction builders may only move one bucket at a time to the construction site.
- Construction managers may not use the terms *line, on top of, front, behind,* or *next to.*
- No one should use put-downs or call other teammates by their last names.
- If any of these rules are broken, the buckets must be returned to the starting area.
- Construction managers must use name of the builder and the name of the bucket when giving instructions. For example, "Wendy, pick up *Integrity* and place it next to *Respect!*"

Possible Solutions

The students are going to have to pick the teammates they feel can give them the best instructions for building the pyramid. The construction managers need to figure out how to best communicate the tower construction without using the words that are prohibited. The team should work together to figure out which bucket the construction managers want to use and where they want it placed. With two construction managers, two builders could be moving at once. See figure 3.13 for a diagram of possible solutions.

Conclusion of Challenge

When the 12 buckets are placed in the correct formation according to the key, the challenge is mastered.

Additions and Variations

- Buckets are marked with a character-education word, its Spanish equivalent, and a number.
  - Build a tower using the English character-education words only.
  - Build a tower using the Spanish words only.
  - The team must build a tower by calling out the only bucket numbers.
- Set a time limit on construction.
- Build a tower using math equations only. For example, use bucket 2 $\times$ 5 – 1 (bucket 9).
- Increase the distance between the starting area and the construction area (the fitness distance), and challenge the team to set a new construction record for their team.

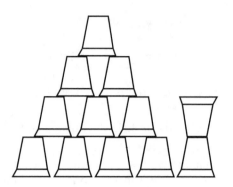

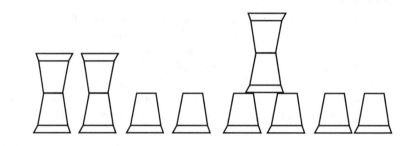

Figure 3.13 Key to Character Cup Stack.

- Construction managers must call out a different way to move each time a bucket is to be delivered to the construction area.
- Construction managers call out a Spanish word, and the builders must call out the English translation before they move the bucket.

For more team-building activities, please see *Team Building Through Physical Challenges* and *More Team Building Challenges*. Both books are from Human Kinetics and provide your class with hours of problem solving for teams.

Remember to incorporate positive adjectives after doing a few challenges.

When your students complete a week of team building, they may start to become closer to their teammates and form a connection to their team. After a week of team building, it will be time for you to start incorporating your own curriculum. The overly competitive students will be more able to tolerate competitive activities, and the highly skilled students will be more able to support their less skilled teammates both physically and emotionally. These challenges enable you to put a premium on social skills before starting competition. This does not make your students less competitive; it only makes them a more cooperative teammate during competition and a more respectful competitor to opponents.

The next chapter, which is on assessment, keeps the connection to physical education strong by continuing the motivational methods needed to encourage an active lifestyle.

Portfolio Assessment

While writing this book, we spoke with dozens of physical educators. It was interesting to hear the attitudes of the teachers in relation to the attitudes of their students. For example, some middle school physical education teachers insisted that no matter what, middle school students did not like physical education. These teachers never thought of evaluating their own program to see if they could do things differently. Instead, they resigned themselves to the fact that this was just a common characteristic of middle schoolers and that there was nothing they could do about it. Basically, they blamed the students.

I brought up portfolios by asking these same teachers if they had ever asked the students what their interests were or what their overall feelings about physical education were. Interestingly enough, the teachers' beliefs were that activities such as discussions and writing reflections or goals take time away from movement—and that's what the students were there for. It soon became clear why their students didn't enjoy physical education.

Their goal was to get as much activity out of the students during their class period. The students were there to be physical; the emotional stuff was a waste of time. The students were never asked how they felt about physical activity or what their interests may be. It didn't matter if the students understood the importance of physical activity or the value of teamwork. What was important was that they were moving as much as possible. They weren't able to explore areas that were of interest to them with the hopes in mind they might participate in those activities on their own time or into their adult lives. As long as they were moving for the whole class period, that's what counted.

We believe teachers with this attitude are doing more harm than good. Many will argue, "Well, for a lot of children, physical education class is the only time they are active." We agree; that is not a good situation and it's very unfortunate. But shouldn't we then focus on helping them develop an emotional connection to physical education in hopes they understand the importance of physical activity and maybe even enjoy it? The Centers for Disease Control and Prevention as well as the National Association of Sports and Physical Education gave recommendations in 1995 and 1997 for physical education programs to include helping students develop the knowledge, attitudes, and skills they need to adopt and maintain a physically active lifestyle (Kulinna et al. 1999).

Assessment is not a separate entity in the teaching and learning process. It is an important concept in creating a safe atmosphere, as well as promoting a continued interest in physical education. In our quest to make physical education a brain-friendly place to be, where students are inspired to exercise, traditional assessment techniques must be changed. Many of these techniques, such as testing students in physical activities they have no interest in, only turn them away from that activity more. Remember Kari in chapter 1? She attributes much of her dislike toward physical activity today to the continued embarrassment she experienced while being assessed in physical education 20 to 30 years ago. Unfortunately, many of those antiquated techniques are still being used today.

In the first part of this chapter, we are going to take a look at why assessment is such a complex issue in education and how it can have a negative effect on students' attitudes towards fitness. The second half of the chapter explores assessment options that truly nurture children's growth and motivation to learn. Specifically in this chapter, you will learn:

- How to incorporate student portfolios into your program
- How to get students more involved in the assessment process by becoming reflective learners
- How to eliminate the threat that often goes along with assessment, while keeping the students' growth and emotional connection to fitness a top priority
- How to foster students' higher-level thinking skills and move away from asking right or wrong questions that only require memorization
- How to focus on the process of learning and growth, rather than the final product

Key Terms

- Self-assessment
- Peer evaluation
- Reflective learning
- Student portfolios
- Rubrics
- Baseline

Assessment is one of the most complex issues in education today. There will never be a perfect way to assess one person versus another, yet many teachers give this concept little thought. What exactly is being measured when assessing another person? Is it how much a person has grown by focusing on the process of learning, or is it a focus on a final product, or "score"?

It seems so easy to just stamp a letter on a report card to reflect the growth or achievement of another person. Does that grade mean the same to one teacher as it does to another? Does it mean the same to the student as it does to the teacher? How important are letter grades to the students, and do they provide incentives for them to do better? Chances are that if 10 teachers were asked these questions, each would come up with different answers.

In my experience as a tutor, I often ask students to bring along their report card after it was issued. When I asked them why they got a certain grade in a particular subject, it was amazing how often I heard, "I don't know." I always follow up with the question, "Do you know what you can do to improve that grade?" The answer was always, "No." This was extremely discouraging to me, and it helped me realize that more often than not, such grades are totally meaningless in whatever purpose they attempt to serve.

Many teachers say that assessment measures a student's growth in a given amount of time. Our response to that is to ask, "What is growth?" How do you measure one person's growth to another's if they each begin at different levels? Each person enters the year or the course at a different level, but so often when grades are issued, they are based at the end of the course on the same system of points or learning curve. In that case, growth or improvement is not what is being considered when only the end product—or "total points" earned throughout the unit, quarter, or semester—is what is being graded on.

Consider, for example, Cathy and Tim. Cathy came to physical education class coordinated and athletic. She loved sports and performed them at a high level. She had a good attitude, and she worked well with others. Tim, on the other hand, was not blessed with athletic ability. He was uncoordinated and performed many skills at a low level, but he tried hard and also worked well with others. By the end of the unit, Tim had improved tremendously, yet he was still only average. Cathy was basically at the same high level from when she started the unit, even though she worked just as hard as Tim. Cathy ended up getting an A, and Tim got a B. Why? Basically, Cathy got a higher grade because of her genetics. In this case, grades weren't used to measure growth. Even if they were used to measure growth, would it have been fair to give Cathy a lower grade because she didn't show as much but still performed at a higher level?

These issues have unfortunately not been given enough thought, as grades have been issued inconsistently from one teacher to another, as well as from school to school and district to district. In addition, the purpose of grades varies so much that it oftentimes ends up being a judgment call made by the teacher.

> In many middle school physical education programs, we have forgotten the intended purpose of grading, and instead, we use it as a means of punishment and rewards. Grading of this kind shortchanges students, whereas a thoughtful assessment plan is likely to cultivate higher-order thinking and problem-solving capacities. You may put a lot of energy into your teaching, but only assessment can tell you if the students are learning.
>
> *Mohnsen, 1998*

Testing may be one way to determine what a student has learned, but testing is overemphasized and has had a negative impact on our educational system. In many cases, traditional testing discourages creativity and ignores the characteristics that are truly important in the success of our children. In 1995, the newsletter *An Odyssey of the Mind* published the top 13 skills desired by Fortune 500 companies. Teamwork was number one. How do knowledge-based tests measure one's ability to work with others? When so much emphasis is placed on test scores, teachers feel pressured to "teach to the test," drilling the students with facts while other more important projects that require working together or individual creativity get shoved aside. The next most important qualities the Fortune 500 desires are as follows:

2. Problem solving

3. Interpersonal skills

4. Oral communications

5. Listening

6. Personal/career development

7. Creative thinking

8. Leadership

9. Goal-setting/motivation

10. Writing

So much emphasis is placed on college entrance exams, such as the ACT and the SAT, and overall GPAs. Because this emphasis comes from the top of the educational system, pressure is put on high schools to cram more and more information into students to better prepare them for these tests. Unfortunately, the pattern continues downward as middle schools and elementary schools are continually pressured to produce higher test scores.

Once students are done with their education, it's interesting how the skills desired by the workplace shift from "How much do you know?" to "How well do you work with others?" It's apparent that either the educational system or the government (the latter of whom mandates certain test requirements) needs to rethink what is truly important in this complex job we have in educating our children.

Because government, colleges, parents, and school districts value grades so highly, teachers are caught in the middle. They do what they believe is right by nurturing the well-being of the whole student versus simply drilling the facts. Good teachers continually struggle with this conflict, fearing that if they don't produce higher test scores, they will be perceived as poor teachers. The easiest way to handle this conflict would be to take the path of least resistance and conform to these external pressures. In that case, teachers should really examine why they chose the teaching profession and the purpose it attempts to serve. We believe that teachers should go with what is in their heart, especially if it is in the best interest of their students. Fortunately, with all the brain research that is influencing education today, assessment is in the process of being transformed into an integral part of education. It will not change, however, unless teachers take the road less-traveled and focus more on the student rather than external pressures.

Reflection is the process of questioning, thinking, determining next actions, and assessing the implication of your actions. Getting students to become reflective in their work—that is, getting them to think about what they have done, what they are doing, and what they are going to do next—is one of the many benefits of student portfolios. Thinking deeper about who they are and how physical education relates to their lives is going to help them establish that emotional connection that is key in developing an appreciation for lifelong fitness. Evaluating their work and developing a plan to improve is much more powerful and meaningful than a teacher's giving a grade with the students' not knowing why they got that grade or what they can do to improve it. In an editorial article about reflection, Kari Dahl (1998) writes: "Through reflection of ordinary experiences, we can gain insights about or regarding our own behaviors, beliefs, and values. We can safely determine if they need changing. We can try small steps to change without anyone but ourselves assessing the results."

Bloom's *Taxonomy* has been around the education world since the 1950s, and it also proves the importance of student portfolios. Very few teachers haven't heard of Bloom, as his work is introduced in almost every teacher-training program in colleges around the United States. Bloom states that knowledge-based questions, often given in the form of multiple choice and true-false tests, require the least amount of brainpower and evaluation; synthesis-based questions, however, require the most. Memorization, recalling, reciting, and defining are what students are doing in typical knowledge-based tests. As a result, much of the information is lost once the test is over because higher-order thinking skills have been set aside to memorize the "facts." Even though this information is as abundant as it is, 80 to 90 percent of the questions teachers ask are still in the knowledge category. Could it be that these types of questions are simply the easiest to score, as they are either right or wrong?

To facilitate a deeper understanding, teachers need to help students reach the synthesis and evaluation level by enabling them to utilize their higher-order thinking skills. Development of opinions, judgments, or decisions are examples of thinking about content and how it relates to their life, rather than just memorizing it. The problem with this type of evaluation, however, is the question, How can a teacher effectively measure someone else's judgments or opinions? Realistically, they can't. So, unfortunately, these type of questions just don't get asked because they are too hard to score. With this in mind, why do teachers have to put a score on everything? Can't students be allowed to give opinions and judgments without the threat of always being judged? The following questions are examples of synthesis- and evaluation-based questions:

- Do you agree that . . . ?
- What do you think about . . . ?
- What is the most important . . . ?
- Place the following in order of priority . . .
- What criteria would you use to assess . . . ?

Say, for example, students were being tested on volleyball. Traditionally, assessment is given via a knowledge-based test with the students' memorizing rules and plays. As a result, the information will be lost once the test is over, unless an emotional connection happens to be made in some other inadvertent way. First, we need to ask, How important is it that they know all the facts about the game in the first place? What if the game means nothing to them and they never play it or watch it for the rest of their lives? It probably is important that they have a general understanding of the game so that they can at least decide if it's important to them and if they want to pursue it further. Instead of facts-based tests, we can facilitate that understanding by assessing them in a way that requires deeper thinking, such as allowing them to make judgments about the game and determine its important aspects. The following questions are examples of a volleyball assessment that includes synthesis- and evaluation-based questions:

1. What do you think are the five most important rules in volleyball? State why you think each one is important.
2. If you could change two rules to make the game more interesting, what rules would you change and why?
3. Do you think volleyball should be an Olympic sport? Why?
4. What is your favorite part of the game?

5. Name three of the skills that you think are the hardest to learn and why.

6. Do you think teams should be required to rotate? Why or why not?

7. If you had the choice, do you think you would ever play or watch this game again?

8. If you had to be one of the following, which would you rather be? A volleyball coach, a volleyball player, or a volleyball referee? Why?

In this assessment, students obviously have to know facts about the game, but they are asked to make judgments about those facts, which requires higher-level thinking skills.

Many teachers would look at these questions and say that there is no way they are going to take the time to assess 150 tests with those type of questions. Our response is, Good! You shouldn't assess other people's ideas and opinions. You could, however, tell if they have a general understanding of the game.

When students are finished taking the test, maybe they could share their answers with their teammates to promote discussion about the game. Again, really hitting on those higher-level thinking skills by being allowed to discuss, compare, judge, and (hopefully) even dispute. Allowing students to discuss by listening to others ideas and sharing their own allow for a nonthreatening, enriching atmosphere. William Glasser (1998) reminds us that we learn:

10 percent of what we read

20 percent of what we hear

30 percent of what we see

50 percent of what we both see and hear

70 percent of what we discuss with others

80 percent of what we experience personally

95 percent of what we teach to someone else

These statistics suggest that students are much more likely to remember what they learned by discussing and working together than they would by working quietly on their own. The hardest part of letting students discuss answers is for the teacher to give up that control. The more students see that the teacher is on their side and doing what's best to help them learn, the more likely students will go above and beyond expectations, instead of taking advantage of the freedom.

If we want students to take an active part in their learning and development, they must be involved in the evaluation process. Reflection is a key component in improving and changing, and it is often taken away from students when someone else is doing the evaluating. Teaching children to become reflective learners is perhaps the biggest benefit of student portfolios. This new way of assessing has become popular in the '90s and has proved to be effective and meaningful. According to Mohnsen (1998) in *Teaching Elementary Physical Education*, "The purpose of these new assessment tools in physical education is to help students move beyond memorization of rules and statistics to the creation of personal practice plans, the development of fitness and wellness programs, and the analysis of their own movement." Empowering students by giving them a voice in their education is invaluable. Students become intrinsically motivated when they know that they are going to be involved, rather than just "judged" by the teacher or graded based on what they scored on a test. Who knows more than the student how much they have improved and how hard they have worked? It seems obvious that they would be part of the process in determining their grade.

Portfolios

Portfolios are a collection of work or performance data that illustrate effort, growth, and achievement. The collection of work can include anything from sharing their personal interests to assessment and evaluation samples. According to Melograno (1998), "Students must be involved in selecting and judging the quality of their own work, including self-reflection. With portfolios, traditional teaching roles may not work. Teachers need to facilitate, guide, and offer choices rather than inform, direct, and predetermine priorities. Partnerships are established among teachers, students and parents." To illustrate these principles, the teacher may say, for example, "Make sure to include at least three self-assessment examples and two peer evaluations." This way, the student could choose the pieces of work they are most proud of.

The key to a successful portfolio, however, is that it must show growth. Many use it simply for a scrapbook, collecting various pieces of work along the unit of study. A key factor in communicating growth is for teachers to instruct students to include a baseline before each new unit of study. We can't tell how far they have come if we don't know where they started.

Benefits of Portfolios in Physical Education

The following are some of the benefits of using portfolios in physical education.

- Helps students track their progress as they strive toward goals that are meaningful to them
- Allows students to better understand their strengths and weaknesses
- Allows students to become reflective learners by focusing on metacognition questions, such as
  - What did I do?
  - How or why did I do it?
  - What did I do well?
  - What can I do to improve?
- Effectively communicates to parents their child's effort and progress
- Engages students in goal setting
- Allows students to focus more on their own individual abilities and growth, as opposed to being compared with others
- Focuses more on the process of growth, improvement, effort, and achievement, rather than just the final product
- Allows students to be involved in their assessment, providing a sense of ownership
- Allows students the opportunity to develop personal health plans

What Can Be Included in a Portfolio?

The following are some of the items that can be included in a portfolio.

- Baseline
- Personal health/fitness reflections or surveys
- Student evaluations/assessment
- Peer evaluations
- Rubrics
- Fitness scores
- Fitness and behavioral goals
- Personal/introduction page

- Scenario reflections
- Parent surveys
- Special assignments or projects
- Journals or logs that track progress throughout the year or unit

Developing a Baseline

This concept is key in determining the growth of an individual. Developing a baseline means determining what knowledge or skills the student begins the unit with. Without doing this, how can teachers determine how much progress an individual has made? By seeing what students know at the beginning of the unit and the end of the unit illustrates just how far they came. The story at the beginning of this chapter about Cathy and Tim shows two examples of very different baselines. Tim began the unit with a low baseline but showed tremendous growth because he had so much room for improvement. Cathy, however, had a much different baseline. She was already functioning at a high level without as much room for drastic improvement.

Developing a baseline can be done a number of different ways. It can be as simple as starting a volleyball unit by having the students state everything they know about volleyball, including specific skills and rules. Another popular way to begin each unit is to have the students create a K-W-L chart (figure 4.1), where they state what they already *know*, what they *want* to know, and at the end of the unit, what they *learned* and how that new learning made them feel. In regular education classes, baselines are the same things as pretests given at the beginning of a unit. It's also important to establish a baseline on attitudes toward the specific unit, as well as social skills such as teamwork and being a good sport. To determine the progress the student has made, the same questions that were asked to develop the baseline at the beginning of the unit should then be asked at the end of the unit.

Developing a skills baseline could be done a number of different ways. For example, students could work with a peer in determining their starting point in a particular unit. For example, in a basketball unit, a teacher may introduce the skill of shooting. After the students develop an understanding of how the shot needs to look and the teacher develops and explains the rubric, the students could practice shooting while a peer evaluates them. They could shoot 10 shots from anywhere they choose. The scorecard could look something like the following Baseline for the Basketball Shot.

Classroom teacher: _____   Your name: _____

Soccer Unit

What do you know?	What do you want to know?	What did you learn?	How did it make you feel?
Know	**Want**	**Learn**	**Feel**

Obtained from the Champlin Park presentations and modified to fit the needs of my students.

Figure 4.1 K-W-L chart.

Baseline for the Basketball Shot

Name of partner: _____

Name of shooter: _____

(Partner fills in the first three blanks below.)

Location of shot: _____

How many shots were made out of 10? _____

Shooting form score: _____ (Based on provided rubrics.)

Why did you give your partner this score? Make sure to include what was done well and what needs to be worked on.

_____

_____

_____

Shooter: What is your goal next time you shoot the same 10 shots?

_____

_____

What are you going to do to try to improve?

_____

_____

If you plan on practicing on your own, you can keep a log of your scores.

____/10   Date: _____

____/10   Date: _____

____/10   Date: _____

____/10   Date: _____

____/10   Date: _____

____/10   Date: _____

From *Character Education* by D. Glover and L. Anderson, 2003, Champaign, IL: Human Kinetics.

The students could practice as often as they like, but to track growth from the beginning of the unit to the end, the same scorecard should be completed by the same partner—except it would look more like the following End of Unit Scorecard.

End of Unit Scorecard

Name of partner: _____

Name of shooter: _____

Location of shot: _____

How many shots were made out of 10? _____

Score of shooting form: _____

Partner: If you noticed any improvement, what improvements were made?

_____

_____

Shooter: What improvements do you feel you have made?

_____

_____

What have you done during this unit to try to improve your shooting?

_____

_____

_____

From *Character Education* by D. Glover and L. Anderson, 2003, Champaign, IL: Human Kinetics.

By including the baseline scorecard and the end of the unit scorecard, it becomes evident if the student has improved in that certain skill.

If a student wants to improve their mile time during a semester, then it would be important to get their mile time both at the beginning and the end. The student could fill out a sheet like the following Baseline Times to keep in their portfolio.

Baseline Times

Name: _____

Distance: _____ Time: _____ Date: _____

Distance: _____ Time: _____ Date: _____

Goal times for the end of the unit:

Distance: _____ Time: _____ Date: _____

What are you going to do to try to improve your time? Example: Are you going to run/walk on your own time? If so, how often and how far? _____

_____

If you do any more time trials before the end of the unit, keep track of them here.

Distance: _____ Time: _____ Date: _____

Distance: _____ Time: _____ Date: _____

Distance: _____ Time: _____ Date: _____

Final Time Trials

Distance: _____ Time: _____ Date: _____

Distance: _____ Time: _____ Date: _____

Distance: _____ Time: _____ Date: _____

Did you improve on your times?   Yes _____   No _____

If you did improve, were you happy with how much?   Yes _____

No _____

What did you do to improve?

_____

How hard do you feel you worked at improving?

_____

If you didn't improve, why not?

_____

From *Character Education* by D. Glover and L. Anderson, 2003, Champaign, IL: Human Kinetics.

Baseline attitudes and knowledge of a sport or activity also should be determined at the beginning of a unit. Examples of baseline surveys are given later in the chapter.

Personal Health/Fitness Reflections and Surveys

These are a great resource to determine baseline and end of unit attitudes. The following examples are ways teachers can develop a better understanding of their students' thoughts and feelings about physical activity. It's amazing how much teachers can learn about their students when they just ask. We can't assume that every student likes physical education nor can we assume that every student dislikes it. We need to give them the opportunity to share how they feel, helping them realize that what they have to say is important. We believe students should be given personal fitness/health reflections at the beginning of the year, quarter, or unit (whatever your situation may be). The purpose is not only for the teacher to get a better understanding of the students but also to get the students to really think about how physical activity fits into their lifestyle.

These also serve as an effective way to determine a student's baseline attitudes. To know whether the student's attitudes and behaviors have changed, the teachers should give the same questions as often as they want, but especially at the end of the year, quarter, or unit. This evaluation is a great tool for the teacher. Obviously, if the students' attitudes aren't changing, then teachers need to take a good, hard look at their program.

In the following sections, we provide a number of ways to get kids to reflect. The following are questions that students could be asked to determine their feelings about physical education. We do not expect teachers to use all of these questions. They serve as merely a guide in hopes that teachers are able to find a few and adapt them to best fit their program.

Physical Education Survey

My favorite things about physical education class are

_____

_____

The things I don't like about physical education class are

_____

_____

_____

Circle how many times you exercise outside of class per week.

  1   2   3   4   5   6   7 or more times

What type of physical activity do you do?

_____

_____

_____

How important do you think exercising is?

_____

If you could change the way things were done in physical education class, what would you change?

_____

_____

_____

Why do you think physical education is important?

_____

_____

_____

From *Character Education* by D. Glover and L. Anderson, 2003, Champaign, IL: Human Kinetics.

Physical Activity Survey

1. List your five favorite activities/games/sports that are taught during the year in your physical education class.

   _____   _____

   _____   _____

   _____

2. I play outside with my friends after school and on the weekends. (Circle one.)

   Most of the time   Sometimes   Seldom

3. The feelings I get from exercising and getting sweaty are

   _____

   _____

4. The first thing I do when I get home from school is

   _____

5. My three favorite activities outside of school are

   _____   _____

   _____

6. I like to participate in physical activities because

   _____

   _____

7. Two of my favorite activities to do with my family are

   _____   _____

8. Describe a typical evening in your house. Tell what you and your family do from the time you get home from school until you go to bed. _____

   _____

   _____

   _____

9. How many sports teams do you play on during the year? ____

From *Character Education* by D. Glover and L. Anderson, 2003, Champaign, IL: Human Kinetics.

10. When I play on an organized team, I have practice ____ nights of the week for about ____ hours each time.

11. Fill in the amount of time (hours, minutes) you spend each day outside of school doing the following:

_____ Homework	_____ Computer
_____ Playing outside in the neighborhood	_____ Reading books
_____ Watching TV teams	_____ Playing on sports
_____ Playing video games	_____ Helping out around the house
_____ Talking on the telephone	_____ Other

From *Character Education* by D. Glover and L. Anderson, 2003, Champaign, IL: Human Kinetics.

Because students have different learning styles, the visual learners may appreciate answering questions in the form of a mind map (figure 4.2), created by Cheryl Fregeau.

Student Evaluations/Assessments

As mentioned earlier, to reach a higher level of understanding, students should regularly have opportunities to evaluate their actions, behaviors, and attitudes. When students engage in metacognition, it allows them to learn more about themselves and how they learn best. Getting students to think about what they did and why they did it enables them to learn more and provides for a better chance of improvement.

For example, teams could have an opportunity to see the final-unit evaluation form or test at the beginning of the unit. They then could discuss and construct the meanings of the questions in their huddles. Obviously, they wouldn't be graded on this, as it is very similar to a pretest. This activity would be characterized as establishing a team baseline. By seeing the evaluation form, they would have an understanding of what they are going to learn during the unit and what things are expected of them.

A powerful way to come up with the unit evaluation or assessment piece is to have the students construct it themselves. Toward the end of the unit, after students have developed a good understanding of important skills and concepts, the teacher could ask, "What do you think you should be graded on in this unit? What skills do you need to have to be successful? What should we be looking for in those specific skills? What are some of the important behaviors and attitudes needed to help in your team's success?"

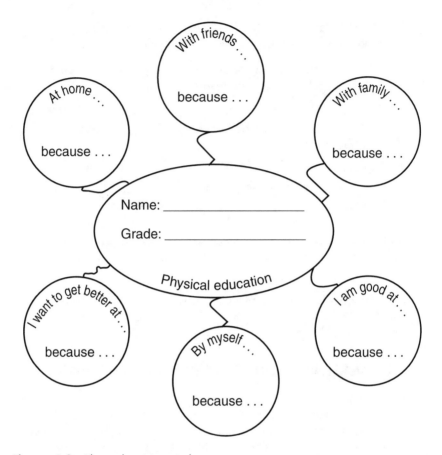

Figure 4.2 Physical activity mind map.

This assignment could be given as a homework and provided as a great way to review what was learned during the unit—while at the same time empowering them by allowing them to say what is on the final evaluation.

Maybe each team could construct their own evaluation form and then consolidate the forms into one. The questions could look like the following.

Final Unit Evaluation

You are going to have the opportunity to help develop the final evaluation for this unit. Please answer the following questions, and I will use the information to create an evaluation for the class.

List five rules that you think everyone should know about this game.

1.

2.

3.

4.

5.

What do you think are the five most important skills that are needed to be successful in this sport?

1.

2.

3.

4.

5.

Out of the five you listed, pick three and list specific characteristics of that skill.

1. _____

   a.

   b.

   c.

   d.

From *Character Education* by D. Glover and L. Anderson, 2003, Champaign, IL: Human Kinetics.

2. _____

    a.

    b.

    c.

    d.

3. _____

    a.

    b.

    c.

    d.

List five additional questions that you think should be included on the final evaluation.

    1.

    2.

    3.

    4.

    5.

From *Character Education* by D. Glover and L. Anderson, 2003, Champaign, IL: Human Kinetics.

The following examples offer many ways to get kids to reflect on their performance. Again, you do not need to use all of them. Choose the questions that relate to what you are looking for, and adapt them to best meet the needs and goals of your program.

General Questions That Can Be Included on Your Unit and Self-Evaluations

1. What unit are you evaluating?
2. Think back on this unit and the skills that were covered. What grade would you give yourself if you were watching yourself play, and why?
3. What did you like about this unit?
4. What did you dislike about this unit?
5. Do you plan on participating in the activities that were included in this unit on your own time? What particular activities do you plan on doing again?
6. What was the most important thing you learned during this unit?
7. Is there anything you wish we would have done more of? Was there anything you think we did too much of?
8. If you were to teach this unit to someone else, what would be the five most important things they would need to know to be successful?
9. In what areas do you feel you have improved (attitude, behavior, physical skills, teamwork, etc.)? Why do you think you improved?
10. In what areas do you hope to improve? How do you plan on improving in these areas?
11. What did you learn in this unit that you feel would help you in future units?
12. On a scale of one to five, with one being *not hard at all* and five being *very hard*, how hard did you work, and why?
13. Describe your attitude during this unit.
14. Do you feel you were a good teammate? Why or why not?
15. Specifically, what were three things you did that displayed good teamwork? Was there anything you did as a teammate that may have hurt your team?
16. Did you encourage or praise any of your teammates? If so, give examples of some of the things you said.
17. In what areas did you work the hardest? Where could you have worked harder?

From *Character Education* by D. Glover and L. Anderson, 2003, Champaign, IL: Human Kinetics.

Team Building Through Physical Challenges

Name: _____

1. I enjoyed the team challenges?   Yes _____   No _____

   Why?
   _____

2. My favorite challenge was
   _____

   Why?
   _____

3. The best thing about my team was
   _____

4. My team could have improved on
   _____

5. What specific feedback did you hear your teammates giving each other? _____

   _____

6. The grade I would give my team is _____.

1	2	3	4	5
Poor		Average		Outstanding

   Why?
   _____

7. The grade I would give myself as a team member is

1	2	3	4	5
Poor		Average		Outstanding

   Why?
   _____

From *Character Education* by D. Glover and L. Anderson, 2003, Champaign, IL: Human Kinetics.

Volleyball Self-Assessment

Name: _____

	Needs work	OK	Good
Specific Skills			
Underhand Serve			
Bumping the ball			
Setting the ball			
Understanding the rules			
Rotation			
Being a good sport			

1. What were my best volleyball skills?

2. Which of my skills do I need to improve most?

3. The things I liked best about volleyball are . . .

4. The things I like least are . . .

5. My overall feeling of volleyball is . . .

6. The grade I think I deserve for effort is: (Circle one.)

> 1   2   3   4   5
>
> Poor   Average   Outstanding

Why? _____

7. The grade I think I deserve for attitude is: (Circle one.)

> 1   2   3   4   5
>
> Poor   Average   Outstanding

Why? _____

From *Character Education* by D. Glover and L. Anderson, 2003, Champaign, IL: Human Kinetics.

Skills Evaluation

(This form could be used for different units.)

1 = I need lots of work at this skill.

2 = I'm doing OK at this skill.

3 = I'm very good at this skill.

4 = I feel I do an excellent job with this skill.

1. Name four specific skills that we've worked on during this unit, and score yourself in each one using the above guide.

   Skill   Score

   _____   _____

   _____   _____

   _____   _____

   _____   _____

2. What characteristics make a good team member and show how to be a good sport? _____

   _____

   _____

3. Do you feel that you were a good team member and that you demonstrated being a good sport?   Yes _____   No _____

   Share specific things you said or did to prove you were or weren't.

   _____

   _____

   _____

From *Character Education* by D. Glover and L. Anderson, 2003, Champaign, IL: Human Kinetics.

Effort and Attitude Self-Assessment

Unit/Activity

3 = Every day   2 = Most days   1 = Not very often

1. I participated to the best of my ability.

    3   2   1

2. I was respectful to all my classmates, the teacher, and the equipment.

    3   2   1

3. My attitude was positive during this unit.

    3   2   1

4. I was in control of my body.

    3   2   1

Total points: _____

5. How would you score yourself overall in good effort and positive attitude?

    3   2   1

    Why?

    _____

Please answer the following questions.

1. What did you enjoy about this unit? (Be specific.)

    _____

    _____

2. What skills do you feel you improved during this unit?

    _____

    _____

From *Character Education* by D. Glover and L. Anderson, 2003, Champaign, IL: Human Kinetics.

Evaluation for Any Team Activity

Teamwork/Being a Good Sport

Instructions: Students, circle the following word that best describes you.

Teacher, circle the following words that best describe the student.

1. I was able to "talk" through any disagreements in a fair and kind manner.

    No   Sometimes   Usually   Yes

2. I argued about calls and decisions made by teammates or the teacher.

    No   Sometimes   Usually   Yes

3. I practiced good teamwork by playing my position.

    No   Sometimes   Usually   Yes

4. I made excuses if I made a mistake.

    No   Sometimes   Usually   Yes

5. I was a kind winner and a gracious loser.

    No   Sometimes   Usually   Yes

6. I enjoyed playing (name of sport) whether my team won or lost.

    No   Sometimes   Usually   Yes

7. I think I improved my (name of sport) skills. (Give examples of specific skills.)

    No   Sometimes   Usually   Yes

8. If my teammates made a mistake, I gave them a dirty look or showed my anger in a different way.

    No   Sometimes   Usually   Yes

Yet another example is the following.

Please rate yourself on how well you performed throughout this unit. In the following categories, circle the number that best represents your performance on a scale of one to five, with one being *poor* and five being *excellent*.

1. No matter what my ability was, I gave 100 percent at all times.

    1   2   3   4   5

From *Character Education* by D. Glover and L. Anderson, 2003, Champaign, IL: Human Kinetics.

2. I gave everyone equal opportunity to have fun!

  1   2   3   4   5

3. I encouraged my teammates/classmates to do their best.

  1   2   3   4   5

4. I controlled my ego. I didn't show off or think that I was the best.

  1   2   3   4   5

5. I demonstrated that I was a good sport.

  1   2   3   4   5

6. I listened to teammates/classmates when they had ideas to share.

  1   2   3   4   5

7. During this unit, I improved in these two areas.

_____ _____

To have more success in this unit, I need to improve in this area.

_____

8. Name three skills in this unit that are used during the course of a game. _____

_____ _____

9. If you were playing a pickup game in this unit, what rules would be useful in allowing for fair play and control of the game? _____

_____

10. Can you become healthier by playing this game? Yes No

11. What are the social benefits of playing this game?

_____

_____

12. If you had to give yourself a grade based on how hard you worked, how much fun you had, what you learned, and how you got along with others, what would that grade be? _____

Why?

_____

From *Character Education* by D. Glover and L. Anderson, 2003, Champaign, IL: Human Kinetics.

What League Are You In?

Circle which one best describes you.

Little Leaguer

Does not follow teacher's instructions.

Disturbs other students during activity.

Feels superior to others.

Does not play safely with equipment or others.

Minor Leaguer

Follows most of teacher's or leader's instructions.

Tries not to disturb other students during activity.

Usually treats everyone equally.

Usually plays safely with equipment and others.

Major Leaguer

Always follows teacher's or leader's instructions.

Always participates in class activity.

Has respect for others in the class.

Always plays safely with equipment and others.

Coach

Is always a Major Leaguer.

Helps teacher with equipment.

Is kind, respectful, and helpful to other students.

Teacher's comments:

_____

Student's comments:

_____

Student's signature: _____

From *Character Education* by D. Glover and L. Anderson, 2003, Champaign, IL: Human Kinetics.

What Is Teamwork?

1. Three important qualities to have to work well in a group are

   _____

   _____

   _____

2. The definition of teamwork is

   _____

   _____

3. Three characteristics that could really hurt a team are

   _____

   _____

   _____

4. Activities I do outside of physical education that require
   teamwork. _____

   _____

5. Five activities or jobs that I may have in the future that require
   teamwork.

   _____

   _____

   _____

   _____

   _____

From *Character Education* by D. Glover and L. Anderson, 2003, Champaign, IL: Human Kinetics.

Peer Evaluations

In peer evaluations, students carry out such roles as partners, observers, and evaluators. Each student assesses his or her peer's performance based on previously stated criteria. In evaluating others, students are forced to think deeply about what they are evaluating, which makes the skill or behavior clearer to them in the process. By watching and evaluating others perform a skill, students could learn just as much as they could from actually practicing the skill itself. Many coaches have their games filmed so that the athletes can watch themselves and their teammates afterward. Seeing what they did right and wrong gives them a better chance of understanding what they need to do to improve.

Peer evaluation can be a powerful learning tool. William Glasser states that we learn 95 percent of what we teach to someone else. Although students may not be specifically teaching the skill to a partner during peer evaluation, they are required to take a much deeper look at that skill and provide feedback that will enable them to improve. The peer evaluator is learning a great deal by evaluating someone else, but it is equally as valuable for the person being evaluated. We are always looking for feedback. Sometimes others see things differently than we see them, and feedback from others is just one more tool to help us get better. We don't always have to agree with the given feedback, but regardless of whether we do or not, we are going to learn from it. Besides, the teacher can only be in one place at one time. When the students know what they should be looking for in a certain skill or assignment, they can make the teacher's job much easier by helping provide the feedback that is so important in improvement.

Peer evaluation enhances student learning by requiring them to interact appropriately with peers. Students are responsible for being fair and accurate with their peer evaluations. Peer evaluations encourage problem solving, develop communication skills, and promote active student involvement. An essential component in effective peer evaluation is that a level of trust is established among peers. Chapter 2 (page 57) provides a reflection scenario and some discussion questions that focus on peer assessment.

It's very important, however, no matter what the peer is evaluating, that the class thoughtfully go over the responsibilities of evaluating someone else's work. This topic is great for a reflection scenario or a huddle activity. The following are examples of discussion questions:

1. What is the purpose of peer evaluation? Why would you evaluate someone else's work?

2. How do you feel when another student is evaluating either a skill that you are performing or work that you completed?

3. What qualities do you want the person who is evaluating you to have?

4. Do you think peer evaluations are fair?

5. What are you going to try to remember when you are evaluating someone else?

6. What is the responsibility of the peer evaluator?

7. If Mark is evaluating Jon's work and if Jon disagrees with what Mark had to say, how could Jon handle that situation?

8. If Bruce is really nervous about a classmate evaluating his jump shot, what could he do?

9. What are the benefits of peer evaluation? What are the downfalls?

Peer evaluation can be a beneficial teaching and learning tool, but it could also be threatening to some by creating possible conflict among classmates. Teachers therefore need to be proactive by discussing these issues before having the students participate in peer evaluation. But another possibility would be to have the students evaluate one another a couple times before discussing the importance of it. This way, students can experience it and be better able to answer the questions thoughtfully.

Hopefully, by discussing peer evaluation as a class or within their huddles, students can realize the importance of fairness and honesty as they construct the meaning and answers to the questions. It's important that the teacher be aware of who is evaluating whom. Maybe the first couple times, students should have the opportunity to pick whom they want to be with in the peer evaluation process. This way, they can feel safe and comfortable. As they get more used to this process, the teacher may begin to assign partners while being aware of who works well with each other. The last thing you would want to happen is a student who feels embarrassed. For example, it may not be a good idea to put the best athlete in the class with the most athletically challenged student. In addition, if some students are just not comfortable being watched while performing a skill or having their work looked over, they should feel safe enough to tell the teacher their feelings and together they could come up with a solution. For example, the teacher could assess them after school, or perhaps the student could perform the skill at home with the parent being the evaluator. Most students, however, are not going to have an issue with peer evaluation. It's important, though, that those who do have other alternatives. Figure 4.3 is an example of a peer- and self-assessment for floor hockey.

For students to effectively evaluate one another, they need to know the criteria (or standards) of the skill they are evaluating. This can be done through rubrics. Students need to understand the predetermined rubrics, or they need to make one up as a class. This again ensures that they know what the skill is supposed to look like.

Rubrics

A rubric is an important guide used for evaluating, and it can be as simple or as detailed as possible. Teachers can develop the rubrics based on what they are looking for in certain skills or behaviors, or the students could

Floor Hockey—Peer Self-Assessment

Name: _____ Date: _____

Partner's name: _____

Hockey Dribbling: Do this on *your own.*

On the signal, practice dribbling the yarn ball. When you hear the stop signal, mark down on the sheet how well you did with the cues listed below.

When dribbling today:	Always	Sometimes	Never
I used small taps			
I bent my knees			
I had control of my ball			
I used both sides of my stick			

Hockey Dribbling: Do this *with* your partner.

Your partner will be observing your dribbling skills. He or she will place an "X" in the appropriate column based on the cues listed below.

When dribbling today my partner:	Always	Sometimes	Never
Used small taps			
Bent his or her knees			
Had control of the yarn ball			
Used both sides of the stick			

Figure 4.3 Floor hockey peer- and self-evaluation.

help create the rubrics. Many resources with rubrics already established are also available to physical education teachers. The article "Six Steps in Developing and Using Fitness Portfolios" (Kulinna et al., 1999) states that after developing the portfolio tasks (the first step), the teacher needs to develop the rubrics (the second step). "Rubrics should represent the important components of each portfolio task. A rubric identifies a set of rules or guidelines at specific levels of performance. They specify the aspects of performance that need to be present in order for students to be assigned a particular score." The following (figure 4.4) is an example of a more detailed rubric to evaluate basketball shots. Next is an example of a much

Basketball Rubrics

Dribbling

+ Always maintained control of ball
  Dribbled great with both hands
  Jogged at a fast speed
  Ball did not go above waist
  Dribbled down and back in a straight line

✓ Maintained some control of ball
  Dribbled good with one hand, okay with the other
  Walked or jogged at a medium speed

− Lost control of ball
  Dribbled okay with one hand, poor with other hand
  Slapped at ball or could not get the ball to dribble
  Ball was above waist
  Moved at a slow speed in a crooked line or too fast to get control

Cone Dribble

+ Maintained control of ball
  Jogged
  Switched hands going around each cone
  Dodged cones

✓ Maintained control of ball most of the time
  Walked
  Switched hands most of the time
  Curved around cones

(continued)

Figure 4.4 Detailed basketball rubric.

Cone Dribble *(continued)*
    Lost control of ball
    Did not switch hands
—   Moved at a slow speed
    Big curves around cones

Passing

Bounce Pass to Partner
    Quick pass from the chest angled to the floor
    Follow-through with arms in direction of pass
+   Ball bounced one time crisply to partner's hands
    Stepped with opposite foot each time

    Slow pass from chest
    No follow-through with arms
✓   Ball bounced one time, partner had to reach for it or it came to his or
      her face
    Stepped with opposite foot some of the time

    Raised arms up and down
—   Ball bounced more than once or bounced too close to partner
    Feet stayed together

Chest Pass to Wall Target
    Quick pass from the chest hit inside the square
+   Follow-through with arms in direction of pass
    Stepped with opposite foot each time

    Slow pass from chest
✓   Little or no follow-through with arms
    Ball touched square some times or came close
    Stepped with opposite foot some of the time

    Raised arms up and down
—   No follow-through with arms
    Ball missed the square completely
    Feet stayed together

Figure 4.4 *(continued)*

Shooting

30 Seconds

+
Made 3 or more baskets and hit rim or backboard the other times
Bent and straightened, used legs for power
Arm follow-through, snapped wrist

✓
Made at least 1 basket, hit rim or backboard most of the time
Pushed the ball up
Forgot to snap wrist or follow-through

−
No baskets made and rarely hit rim or backboard
Held ball below waist or above head to shoot
Did not bend knees or elbows

Basketball Report

Dribbling

Down and back/switching hands ____

Cone dribble/switching hands ____

Passing

Bounce pass to partner ____

Chest pass to wall target ____

Shooting

30 seconds/form ____

Made baskets   Hit backboard   Hit rim

Game Play

Used skills ____

Followed and understood rules ____

Sportsmanship ____

Self-Evaluation

Rate yourself

Skills _____

Sportsmanship _____

Basketball Report

Dribbling

Down and back/switching hands ____

Cone dribble/switching hands ____

Passing

Bounce pass to partner ____

Chest pass to wall target ____

Shooting

30 seconds/form ____

Made baskets   Hit backboard   Hit rim

Game Play

Used skills ____

Followed and understood rules ____

Sportsmanship ____

Self-Evaluation

Rate yourself

Skills _____

Sportsmanship _____

Figure 4.4   *(continued)*

Basketball Shot Rubric

	4	3	2	1
Balance	Feet shoulder width apart, shooting foot slightly forward, extends legs as shot is taken	Feet shoulder width apart, shooting foot not designated	Large forward stride when shooting	Feet close together, no stride with shot
Elbow	Elbow held in at approximately 90 degree angle, shooting hand under the ball	Elbow held in but tucked in low to body, shooting hand under the ball	Elbows out, shooting hand designated before shot but rotates into two-hand shot	Elbows extending out to side, no shooting hand designated (two-hand shot)
Eyes	Eyes fixed on the rim until the ball arrives	Eyes fixed on the rim when shot is taken	Eyes fixed on rim when the ball is shot, but then follows the flight of the ball	Doesn't look at rim before shooting the ball
Follow-through	One-hand shot, nonshooting hand used to stabilize the ball, holds follow-through after shot	One-hand shot, nonshooting hand used to stabilize the ball, does not hold the follow-through after the shot	Two-hand shot, but holds follow-through after shot	Two-hand shot, no follow-through

Figure 4.5 Simple basketball rubric.

simpler rubric, developed by elementary physical education teacher Jennifer Youngquist (figure 4.5).

Rubrics make it much easier for peers to evaluate one another. By having a rubric in hand and by understanding what they are looking for, students can successfully evaluate others while learning more about the skill in the process. Figure 4.6 illustrates a bowling rubric.

When I first taught the skill of the basketball shot to a college class, I showed them exactly what the shot should look like. I used the term BEEF. I first explained *balance* and showed them what it should look like; then I taught them how to use their *eyes* and *elbow;* finally, I demonstrated what the *follow-through* should look like. When I was finished with the demonstration, I told them we were going to score the shot using *three-two-one.* I asked them, "If you were to get the highest score on your shot, a *three,* what would it have to look like?" They then explained back to me the standard for a shot that was a *three.* We then did the same for a *two* and a *one.* In that short time, they reviewed exactly what a shot should look like and developed a rubric in the process. This particular lesson was effective, but perhaps the most positive aspect of the lesson was the ownership they felt in creating the standards on which they were going to be evaluated.

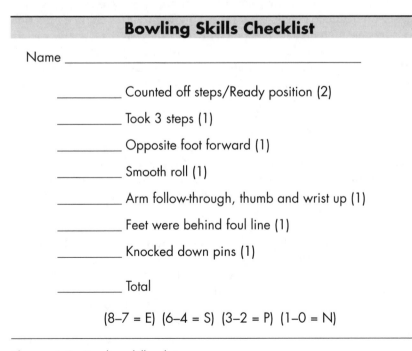

Bowling Skills Checklist

Name _____

_____ Counted off steps/Ready position (2)

_____ Took 3 steps (1)

_____ Opposite foot forward (1)

_____ Smooth roll (1)

_____ Arm follow-through, thumb and wrist up (1)

_____ Feet were behind foul line (1)

_____ Knocked down pins (1)

_____ Total

(8–7 = E) (6–4 = S) (3–2 = P) (1–0 = N)

Figure 4.6 Bowling skills rubric.

This was about a 20-minute process. Students then took 10 shots from wherever they wanted while their peer evaluated them, which could also have been how each student came up with a baseline. (See the Baseline for the Basketball Shot form on page 165.)

Fitness Scores

Fitness scores include results from any type of testing that takes place. Teachers may require all tests to be included in the portfolio, or they may require a certain number. For example, if there are eight tests given during a semester, the teacher may require the students to include five or six of them. This privilege allows students the choice of including the tests they are most proud of.

Fitness Goals

If students set goals for themselves in physical education class and develop plans on how they are going to reach those goals, they will become much more motivated to exercise outside of class time. When students set goals, teachers should always ask the question, "What are you going to do on your own time to help reach this goal?" What they do on their own time could be considered their practice goal, and they should have a specific plan for it. The lesson is that it is not only important to have an ultimate goal but also a process goal. For example, "To reach my goal of 15 laps by the next Heart Healthy Day, I will walk or run 30 minutes, 5 days a week." The plans students develop can be called their Individual Fitness Plans (IFP). (In regular education classes, some students have what is called an Individual Education Plan, or IEP.)

Each plan is unique to each student, and each maps out a specific path to follow to ensure success. IEPs are made up for the student by the educators; IFPs are made up by the students for themselves. Students could create these at the beginning of the unit after a baseline has been determined. Once students see their starting point or baseline, they have a much clearer vision of where they hope to be at the end of the unit. Once they determine that goal, it becomes easier to develop the plan of action toward reaching it. Students should then give themselves a grade at the end of the unit, based on how well they followed their plan. Teachers should also be aware of each student's plan, as should a peer or fitness buddy. The teacher and fitness buddy can sign their names once the plan is created, indicating they are aware of the IFP and will encourage that student to do their best to follow it.

Because so many skills are addressed throughout the unit, it would take forever for the students to develop an IFP for every skill. So give students a choice as to which skills are most important to them. They are more likely to practice on their own time if they are working toward something that had meaning to them.

Each year, physical educator Jennifer Youngquist creates a list of physical activities that her class will participate in throughout the year. She puts them in spreadsheet form and makes a copy for each student (figure 4.7) The purpose of this is to get kids to practice outside of school, as well as work on predicting performance and setting goals. Students record their prediction of how many times they will be able to do a specific task. They then perform the skill, and their partner records their score and writes in their initials. Next, the students each set a goal for that task that they will work toward during that unit. For example, at his first try, Tom estimates he can jump rope 50 times in one minute. His partner Jeff times him and counts. Jeff counted 46 jumps, recorded the score, and initialed it. Tom's goal that he set for the end of the eight-week unit was 65. This gave Tom something he could work toward and practice at home.

Fitness Buddies

To promote working together and working outside of class, teachers can assign each student a fitness buddy (figure 4.8). The purpose of the fitness buddy is for students to support and encourage their partner as they work toward the goals they have set. For example, if Cade sets a goal to engage in physical activity for 30 minutes, 5 days a week, he should show his fitness buddy, Micheal. Micheal can then sign Cade's goal sheet to indicate he is going to support Cade in the pursuit of his goal. Micheal could check up on Cade as often as possible to check progress and to praise and encourage him as needed. Students could come up with the responsibilities of the fitness buddy by constructing guidelines.

It is also a good idea to encourage students to get together outside of class to work on their goals. It's always easier to get up and exercise when having a friend to talk to. Ultimately, what we want is for students to exercise on their own time. Because they are more apt to do so when their fitness buddy is a friend, we believe students should be allowed to pick their fitness buddy. It's important, however, that the teacher be aware of who may be left out by possibly having a plan for those students to join another group. Is it okay for students to have more than two in a group? Our answer is to that is, of course—whatever it takes for students to be more likely to engage in activity outside of class. The fitness buddies are something that the teacher needs to be flexible on. Fitness buddy rules certainly don't need to be cut and dry; they are merely another tool that encourages students to be active.

Partner Physical Activity Check-Off Sheet

Name

Skill challenge	Estimate	Actual	Initial	Goal	Actual	Initial
How many times can you jump rope in 1 minute?						
Can you jump rope for 30 seconds without a miss?						
How many baskets can you make in 1 minute?						
How long will it take you to dribble down and back?						
How many sit-ups can you do in 1 minute?						
How many crab kicks can you do in 1 minute?						
How long will it take you to complete 1 mile?						
Can you hula hoop around your waist for 30 seconds?						
How many times in a row can you and your partner toss and catch a ball?						
How many ups can you do with a racket in 1 minute?						
How many downs can you do with a racket in 1 minute?						
How many times in a row can you and your partner volley a volleyball?						

How many times can you set the ball or balloon to yourself in 1 minute?							
How many times can you kick a soccer ball against a wall with your right foot in 1 minute?							
How many times can you kick a soccer ball against a wall with your left foot in 1 minute?							
How far can you punt a ball?							
How far can you throw a ball?							

Figure 4.7 Partner physical activity check-off sheet.

Figure 4.8 Fitness buddies.

Scenario Reflections

Although we have talked about scenario reflections being given in the form of discussion prompts, teachers can use them in other ways. For example, instead of having kids discuss the situation, they can write down their responses to the questions individually. When the class seems to be struggling in a certain area, the teacher could find a scenario reflection that relates to the situation and have everyone fill it out individually before discussing it.

Another possibility would be when a particular student has problems in a certain area. The teacher could have the student fill out a scenario reflection specific to the student's conflict. For example, Tony is one of the better athletes in the class, and he continually brags about his abilities. The teacher may have him fill out the scenario reflection Good Athlete; Bad Teammate in chapter 2 on page 60.

After Tony writes down his responses, the teacher could go over them with him to see if what he wrote is consistent with what he does. It is very important, however, that this exercise be viewed not as a punishment but rather as an opportunity to reflect and consider. The minute students view it as a punishment, they react negatively to the conversation. Remember

Heart Healthy Goal Sheet

Name: _____

Date: _____

Activity: _____

As a result of your heart rate at the first checkpoint, did you have to change your pace? Why and how did you change? _____

_____

_____

Was your heart rate where you wanted it to be at the second check point?_____

What does this tell you?_____

For Walking, Running, and Swimming

What was your goal for today?_____

_____

How many laps did you get in today? _____

Why or why not did you reach your goal?_____

_____

Write a practice goal (optional). Example: I will walk for 20 minutes five out of seven days a week.

_____

_____

Who is your fitness friend who will encourage you and with whom you will share your goal?_____

_____

Goal for next Heart Healthy day:

_____

_____

_____

_____

From *Character Education* by D. Glover and L. Anderson, 2003, Champaign, IL: Human Kinetics.

chapter 1, when we discussed the fight-or-flight behaviors. Those behaviors kick in when the students feel threatened in any way. It is much more productive when the discussion takes place in a nonthreatening, caring atmosphere, with the teacher questioning the students, not accusing them!

In addition to these reflection scenarios, goal-setting forms, and assessments, the following portfolio additions will help to make the student's portfolio something to be proud of.

Personal/Introduction Page

Students should have the opportunity to decorate the portfolio in a way that best describes them or create a personal introductory page. Cheryl Fregeau, physical education teacher in Anoka, Minnesota, used portfolios with her seventh-grade classes. She took a picture of each child, posing in a favorite sport, so that they could all place their picture on the cover of their portfolio. To make this task easier, a parent could easily come in, take the pictures, then get them developed. Students could put their favorite inspirational quote on the cover along with pictures of some of their favorite sports or athletes.

Jennifer Youngquist had her students decorate the cover of their portfolios with their hopes, wishes, and dreams (figure 4.9). In the follow-

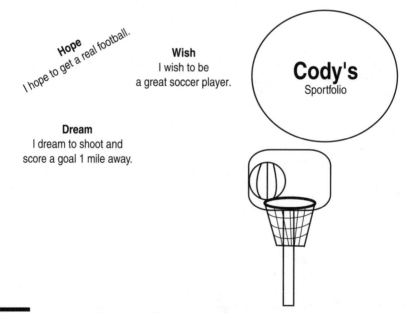

Figure 4.9 Portfolio cover of a young student.

ing example, Cody hopes to get a real football; he wishes to be a great soccer player; and he dreams to shoot and score a goal from one mile away.

Parent Feedback

Portfolios are not only a great way to communicate to parents the growth of their child; they are a great way to involve the parents as well. As stated earlier, parents could be part of the evaluation process in special projects that provide feedback to their child. They could also be evaluators at home for when students need help or just need someone to time them or count how many times they can jump rope in one minute. The following letter was sent home by Cheryl Fregeau, a physical education teacher in Anoka, Minnesota.

Dear Parents of 6th Graders,

This is a PE portfolio your child has been working on in my class for the past nine weeks. I chose one class to implement this new way of assessing and evaluating. Portfolios are designed to allow students the opportunity to demonstrate the things they are learning in PE and to share their feelings about those activities. I have tried to involve them in the process of self-evaluating and even peer assessing skills in groups. Portfolios also give you parents more information about what your child is doing in class. I will be sending these home each quarter for you to look through and provide feedback as to what you learned about your child. If you have any questions, please let me know. Thank you!

This was Cheryl's first year using portfolios, and she started with small steps by choosing certain grade levels to implement them into. Also, because she only had conferences twice a year, she sent home portfolios quarterly so that parents could see their child's progress.

Parents should be encouraged to fill out a questionnaire indicating what they learned about the portfolios. It could look something like the one on the next page.

Teachers must remember that their students can't make their parents fill out this form. As a teacher, you can only remind the students to bring back the form once their parents have filled it out. In Cheryl's case, she got back

Parent Portfolio Feedback Form

1. What did you learn about your child while looking through the portfolio?

   _____

   _____

2. What were you most proud of?

   _____

   _____

   _____

3. What surprised you the most?

   _____

   _____

   _____

4. Could you tell if your child made progress in any particular area?

   _____

   _____

   _____

5. What would you like to say to your child about the work they have done in physical education this quarter?

   _____

   _____

   _____

From *Character Education* by D. Glover and L. Anderson, 2003, Champaign, IL: Human Kinetics.

all but two responses from her class. Cheryl teaches in a private school where parent involvement is high, which won't be the case in all schools, so it's important not to make the students feel bad if any of their parents won't fill out the form. Remember, the students are only the messengers. Don't add insult to injury by getting frustrated at them. They probably feel bad enough that their mom or dad won't take the time to fill out this form. For the most part, however, parents are happy to be involved with their children's learning—many of them simply don't know how—but most will be thrilled that they are asked to provide feedback regarding their child's growth.

Encouraging Parent Involvement in Your Class

Other than track-and-field day, rarely do you see a parent volunteer in physical education. Parents are often so willing to help that we just don't always know how to use them. The following are additional ways parents could help out:

- **Supervising.** If not all students are in the same place, parents could then supervise. Teachers would have to make sure to get this approved by the principal first.

- **Organizing portfolios.** This task can sometimes take more time than a teacher would want to spend. Parents are more than happy to help out in this capacity.

- **Setting up and taking down.** So much time is spent on this. Think of the time that could be saved with good help.

- **Hanging posters throughout the gym.** If each class comes up with their own set of rules or characteristics of certain words, it's important to display their work. Displaying their work as opposed to store-bought posters would again create a sense of ownership; however, it takes a lot of time. This is a great possibility for those parents who are always looking to help.

- **Scheduling speakers.** If the physical education teacher doesn't want to take the time to set up outside resources, it's very likely a parent would be willing to help in this area. It would be a very powerful message for students to hear personally from men and women who changed their lifestyles as a result of a heart attack from smoking or lack of exercise. Other possibilities include nurses, dieticians, and doctors who could speak on their experiences with lung cancer, obesity, and heart disease. If teachers don't want to use physical education time for this, perhaps the language-arts teacher would allow class time for this valuable message.

Special Assignments/Projects

A great way to get students involved while building their character and leadership skills is to have them create their own team talks, inspirational sayings, and warm-ups. Each child could be responsible for coming up with one or two out of the three possibilities. For example, they could write their own inspirational saying or bring in their favorite, or they could provide questions that would facilitate discussion in team huddles.

Another option that students could choose is to create their own team talk or scenario reflection, along with discussion questions. With this option and the creation of the inspirational saying, students would have to get the approval of the teacher before facilitating their work in the huddle activities. Finally, the last option would be for the students to create a warm-up to lead the class. The students would have to provide a lesson plan for the teacher that shows they understand the purpose of a warm-up as well as the movements the students are going to be practicing. The lesson plan could look like the following.

Warm-Up

1. What is the purpose of a warm-up? _____

_____

2. How does the class need to be set up before the warm-up begins—individually, with partners, or in teams? _____

_____

What are the instructions you are going to give to get the class set up that way? _____

_____

3. What is the class going to do for the warm-up? _____

_____

What instructions are you going to give for them to understand what you want them to do? _____

_____

4. How long will each part of the warm-up take? _____

_____

5. Where did you get the idea for this warm-up? _____

_____

6. How are you going to make sure everyone hears what you are saying? _____

_____

From *Character Education* by D. Glover and L. Anderson, 2003, Champaign, IL: Human Kinetics.

Before any of the students lead the warm-up, the teacher needs to look over this sheet to make sure they know exactly what they will be doing.

After the students lead the class through their selected activity, they should fill out a reflection sheet based on how they thought the activity went. It could look something like the following.

1. What activity did you facilitate the class through?
2. How were you feeling before you got started?
3. Explain how you think the activity went.
4. What do you think went well?
5. What do you wish you could've changed?
6. Would you like to facilitate the class through an activity again? Why or why not?

The teacher could also add comments to the student's reflection. These could be included in their portfolio and communicated to parents as (hopefully) something they are proud of. Again, the teacher could require only one of these activities from the students, or all of them. Perhaps students could be required to complete them all but have the choice as to which one they want the facilitator to include in their portfolio.

Portfolio Final Project

Another alternative to the knowledge-based test at the end of a unit is to assign a final project, which could be done outside of class. The assessment of the projects, however, may take up more time than physical education teachers want to give. We are not suggesting a final project be used every unit—maybe just once or twice per year, depending on the teacher and the class situations. For example, an elementary physical education teacher may assign fifth graders just one project a year and perhaps can share those projects with other grades. For example, they may have to make up their own game or team-building challenge, then teach it to a group of first or second graders. The rest of the grades would soon learn that when they get into fifth-grade physical education, they will have the opportunity to create an exciting project that they too will be able to share with the rest of the school.

A high school physical education teacher may require each student to complete one project during the semester. For example, if students participated in three different units during a semester, they could choose which unit they would like to do a project on. The following are examples of different projects students could complete for the unit of volleyball.

1. If you were a high school coach, what would your first week of practice look like? Please include each day's practice plan with the following details, describing why you chose the activities you did: time schedule, specific drills, focus for the day, thought for the day, and rationale for each day.

2. The school board in your district has to make cuts, and volleyball is one of the sports that may go. Prepare a presentation for the board that either supports their decision to cut volleyball or argues their decision in hopes that it will not be cut. Your presentation should include the following: five facts about the game, five interviews, two statistics, and your personal opinion of the game, backed by experiences and examples.

3. Modify the game. If you could make up your own game that you think would be similar but better than volleyball, what would it look like? Include the following: at least 10 rules, keeping 4 of the current rules; at least 3 current skills, along with 4 new ones; a name for your new sport; any necessary specific equipment. Create a list that states the top five characteristics a player would need to have to be successful.

4. As a final option, students can create their own project—with the teacher's approval, of course.

To encourage cooperation, discussion, learning, and motivation, teachers could give students the choice of whether they want to work with another person. It's important that projects be presented in some way, but obviously time is an issue. The following are suggestions on ways projects could be presented.

Project Presentations

1. Have students present their projects to their teammates in their huddles. Set aside five minutes per class period during the last two weeks of the unit. During each of those class periods, one or two students could present in each huddle. That way, 5 to 10 students could present each class period (this number, of course, depends on how many students are presenting with partners and how many teams a class has). The question then becomes, How can the teacher observe each presentation? This can be done in several ways. First, maybe the teacher doesn't need to be at each presentation for the whole time. The teacher could walk around and get as much information as possible but also rely on the students to give an honest assessment of their own project, then the teacher could take a closer look when the

project is actually handed in. Many physical education teachers do not want to take the time to sit down and correct 150 projects. With the informal observation, the student's self-assessment, and possibly a peer assessment, the teacher wouldn't have to take a lot of time looking over each one.

2. While the rest of the class is participating in warm-ups or activities, pull aside a team and have them do their presentations. This ensures that the teacher gets to observe each one.

3. Have the students present their projects to other classes, spreading the word about the unit of study. For example, fifth graders could present to second or third graders, which could be done by having the fifth grader visit the younger students' physical education class. Or, the fifth grader could visit their homeroom class while the classroom teacher observes the presentation.

4. The projects could be presented in language arts class. This option would probably be in an elementary setting, as students stay together for a large portion of the day. Not only is this a great language arts activity, but it's also a great way to connect the two disciplines.

5. If there is not a time-efficient solution for presentations during any class period, the students could have the option of setting up the time and audience to whom they could give their presentations. For example, the presentation requirement could be stated as follows:

> You will be responsible for presenting your projects. It is up to you to set the time of your presentation and to present to at least four people, one of those being an adult. In finding your audience, you will need to provide an invitation that states the date, time, location, and a brief summary of your presentation. The invitation needs to be handed in with your project. Each person in attendance needs to fill out an evaluation form to provide feedback on your presentation. These evaluations also need to be turned in with your project. People you could invite to your presentation include peers, parents, relatives, neighbors, older brothers and sisters, coaches, and family friends.

Evaluating Projects

A rubric has to be established before the projects begin. One way to do that is to have teammates create one in their huddles, then the teacher could use their suggestions to make the final one—again empowering the students by giving them a voice. Ask the students, "How should these projects be graded? If these projects were worth 50 points, how would you break down the points? What important aspects of these projects should be graded, and how much should each aspect be worth?" Or, the teacher could say,

> What would these projects have to look like to get an A? To get a B? Think about it over the next couple days. When we meet again, you and your teammates will have the opportunity to create a rubric to determine how your projects should be graded. I will use your suggestions to create the final rubrics.

Obviously, students would have to know what a rubric is and understand the purpose of it.

Maybe developing a rubric could be homework for the students: "By the next class period, I want you to turn in a rubric that describes how you think these projects should be graded. Include what an A would look like, what a B would look like, and so on. If the rubric is based on a points system, describe what would be worth how many points." Why not give the students the option of working with a partner while coming up with these rubrics—again, promoting discussion and catering to the different learning styles. Teachers may have a hard time with the concept of letting students work with others. They may think that students will take advantage of this freedom. Those students, however, are the minority, and why should the rest of the class have to suffer the consequences because two or three students are going to abuse the trust given to them. After a while, students start to speak up to one another and hold each other accountable, especially if the atmosphere is safe and one in which the trust has been built between the teacher and students.

Self-Assessment

Students should have an opportunity to evaluate their own projects by using the predetermined rubric to determine their final grade. Other questions that could be asked on their final evaluation include the following:

1. On a scale of one to five, one being *not hard at all* and five being *very hard*, how hard did you work on your project?____ Why did you rate yourself that way?
2. What did you enjoy most about completing this project?
3. What were some of the most important things you learned?
4. What was the hardest thing about completing this project?
5. Did you work on this project alone or with a partner? Why?
6. What was the hardest part about working with a partner or working alone?

7. What was the best part about working with a partner or working alone?

Parent Evaluation

A way to get the parents involved would be to have them also fill out an evaluation. The goal here would be for the parent and child to sit down together and go over the project. Parents could be given a simple evaluation form that allows them to provide feedback rather then assessment. The following is an example of a letter to parents asking them to share some of their thoughts regarding their child's project.

Dear Parents/Guardians,

The last few weeks your child has been working on a project for physical education. The projects are due _____. Before your child turns in the project, I would like you to give them some feedback as to how well you think they did. Please take a few minutes to go over the project with your child, then answer the following questions. I would like these evaluation forms by _____. Thank you very much and enjoy the projects!

1. What did you learn about the unit after going over the project with your child?
2. What did you learn about your child?
3. What part of the project are you most proud of?
4. How hard do you think your child worked on this project?
5. Is there anything that surprised you?

Parent's signature: _____

Student's signature: _____

Date: _____

From *Character Education* by D. Glover and L. Anderson, 2003, Champaign, IL: Human Kinetics.

Peer Assessment/Evaluation

Peers should have a chance to evaluate each other's projects. More learning takes place when students are allowed to look over one another's work and provide thoughtful feedback. The evaluator could actually give a grade based on the predetermined rubric. The teacher may look at what the students gave themselves for a final grade, as well as what the peer gave them. If they are similar, great! If they vary greatly, the teacher would have to look the project over a bit more carefully. The peer feedback form could look something like this:

- What did you learn from this student's project?
- What did this student do well?
- What improvements do you think this student could make?
- Do you question anything this student did?
- Based on the rubric for this project, what do you think the final grade should be? Why?

Teacher Evaluation

The teachers would obviously want to have a final say in the evaluation. The big change here, though, is that they aren't going to be the only one having the say—it's a partnership. More often than not, teachers who have allowed students to give themselves grades find the students are typically harder on themselves than the teacher would be. Teachers who haven't attempted sharing the evaluation process with their students often fear it would be the opposite, with most students giving themselves better grades then they deserve. When there is a discrepancy between the student and the teacher regarding what the student deserves, they simply talk about it. Together, they come up with an agreement in what the final grade should be. Again, teachers who haven't experienced this process would argue that this would take up so much time, having to conference with so many students. When the right environment is created and the students feel they can genuinely trust the teacher, very few conferences will have to take place. When they do, they do not need to take long. The students would basically state their reasons, as well as provide evidence through their portfolio, as to why they deserve a certain grade. The teacher would then give reasons for the grade, and (hopefully) the two parties could easily come to an agreement. Again, situations like these are the minority. The responsibilities of self-assessing would also be a great subject for a team talk. (See chapter 2, page 56.)

Journals or Fitness Logs

Students could keep journals or fitness logs throughout the year to track their progress. When the teacher wants to encourage activity outside of class, it's a good idea to give the students fitness challenges and let them set goals and keep track of what they are doing through these journals or logs. In regular education classes, a teacher may have the students keep track of a reading log, journaling how long they read and what they read each day. Many teachers set reading goals for the number of minutes their class reads. Why can't the same activities be done in physical education? A letter could be sent home to parents stating something like this:

Dear Parents/Guardians,

Just as your child has daily homework to exercise the brain, I am assigning homework to (just as importantly) exercise the body. Childhood disease as a result of inactivity is at an all-time high. To promote good health and good habits, I am asking your child to exercise for 30 minutes, at least five days a week. Each student has a fitness log where they can keep track of their daily activity. If they are already involved with after school sports, then that will fulfill the requirement. Other possible activities they could engage in include walking, running, tennis, playing tag, raking, mowing the lawn (with a manual mower), swimming . . . the list goes on. Be creative and have fun! See how long it takes your child to run a certain course. Take note of their fastest time, and let them run it as often as they want to try and beat their time.

Your child and I thank you in advance for your support and encouragement in this pursuit of good health.

Running/Walking Club

Teachers could establish a running/walking club throughout the school by mapping out a course on the school property. Students could keep track of their totals in a classroom log and set a goal to "run across America." A classroom representative could be responsible for adding up the totals in their class and recording them on the master chart in the gym. Student representatives could change weekly, and they could also be responsible for getting school totals each week to track the route. Progress could be announced weekly over the loud speaker as to how far they have run. Once this program gets going, the teacher can easily turn the responsibilities over to students. A running/walking club is a great way for students to get in their 30 minutes a day while they work toward individual and school goals.

A group of teachers out of the Anoka-Hennipen school district in Minnesota came up with the following calendar (figure 4.10a), creatively giving students ideas for daily activity. The students were responsible for keeping track of their activity, and at the end of the month, they were assessed based on the provided rubric (figure 4.10b).

Organization of Portfolios

To help students organize their portfolio, the teacher should have a list of required portfolio contents, as well as the order the contents should be in. By having a specific order, it is easier to go through the portfolios at conferences. In addition, the portfolio should show growth; therefore, the order should be similar to the units done in class. For example, the baselines should be before any other work that pertains to the skills learned throughout the unit.

Portfolio Requirements
Each unit needs to have the following:

- Introduction page
- Interest survey
- Skills and attitude baseline
- Self-assessments (2)
- Peer evaluations (2)
- Fitness skills scores with improvement goals (2)
- Final grade and self-assessment for unit
- Fitness log
- Anything else the students are proud of

The students keep all of their work in their portfolio throughout the unit. Teachers should give time once or twice a month to organize and update portfolios. Elementary students could possibly work on them during language arts or study time. (That would only be possible if the class stays together for a portion of the day because the portfolios could then be transported together from teacher to teacher, thus reducing the risk of losing anything.)

Older students may ask to take their portfolios home to organize them, but again, there is a slight chance things may get lost. Because portfolios have to be managed carefully, teachers need to find a system that works best for them.

Muscular March Madness 2001

Sensible Sunday	Muscular Monday	Tummy Tuesday	Winded Wednesday	Stretch and Tone Thursday	Praise Phrase Friday	Sharing Saturday
• Eat veggies • Eat fruit • Drink milk • Drink water • Healthy snacks	• Push-ups • Pull-ups on monkey bars • Swinging across monkey bars	• Curl-ups • Crunches • Sit-ups • Superstar stretch	• Jogging • Walking • Jump rope • Ride bike • Play tag • Play a sport	• Sit and reach • Hurdle stretch • Toe touches • Windmills • Reach for sky	• Give a compliment • Encourage someone • Say "please" and "thank you" • Give a high-five	• Talk to an adult • Call a friend • Write a letter • Help a neihbor • Act of kindness
				1	2	3
4	5	6	7	8	9	10
11	12	13	14	15	16	17
18	19	20	21	22	23	24
25	26	27	28	29	30	31

Under each day is an example of an activity you could do for that day. Choose one or create your own. Write in the activity you complete. Have fun and remember to treat your body well. It's the only one you get!

Figure 4.10a Sample calendar for student daily activities.

Rubric Calendar Part B Task 2 Elementary Physical Education	
4	**3**
In showing evidence of participating and recording in a daily fitness plan, the student . . . • Participates in a daily fitness plan and records his or her performance 90-100% of the time, hands fitness plan in. • Consistently participates in additional daily physical activities, must be logged on fitness plan. • Logs duration of each activity.	In showing evidence of participating and recording in a daily fitness plan, the student . . . • Participates in a daily fitness plan and records his or her performance 80-89% of the time, hands fitness plan in.
2	**1**
In showing evidence of participating and recording in a daily fitness plan, the student . . . • Participates in a daily fitness plan and records his or her performance 70-79% of the time, hands fitness plan in.	In showing evidence of participating and recording in a daily fitness plan, the student . . . • Participates in a daily fitness plan and records his or her performance less than 70% of the time, hands fitness plan in.
Zero	

Figure 4.10b An assessment rubric.

Start Small!

Teachers who implement portfolios for the first time almost always give this advice. For example, an elementary school physical education teacher may want to implement them for the first time just with fifth graders, or a secondary teacher may want to implement them just for the volleyball unit. Let's say that a teacher has two sections of volleyball per quarter. By the second quarter, the teacher has a chance to change things that didn't go well and continue with the things that did. By the fourth quarter, the teacher should have it down pretty well.

Evaluation of the Portfolio

Evaluation is probably the most challenging aspect of this whole portfolio process. Just like the project assessment explained earlier, the portfolio should be assessed with a predetermined rubric. The teacher first needs to decide on what components to base a grade. Is it going to be on the growth communicated through the portfolio, as well as the quality of the portfolio itself? Teachers ultimately have to find a system that works best for them. They may even have a final test in the portfolio, which can be weighed in determining the final grade.

In talking with teachers about evaluating their portfolios, we concluded that there was obviously no right or wrong way. The most common phrase was simply . . . "keep it simple." Some teachers used the portfolio mainly as a means to communicate to the parents what their child is doing through the collection of work and test samples. Contents in the portfolio may have been used to determine the final grade; however, the final grade wasn't specifically on the whole portfolio.

Whatever system a teacher chooses to use, the students must be part of the process. For every grade or evaluation the teacher gives, the students should be giving themselves one as well. If the grades are similar, which is often the case, then great—you have a final grade. However, if they are different, the teacher and student must take some time to conference and explain to each other why they gave the grades they did. The following is an example of how a final grade could be determined.

Do you have the following pieces of work in your portfolio?

- Unit baseline
- Unit goal
- IFP (Individual Fitness Plan)
- Peer evaluation
- Self-assessment
- IFP final reflection
- Final unit evaluation and grade

Self: Yes _____ (sign)
No. What's missing? Why is it missing?

Peer: Yes _____ (sign)
No. What's missing?

A – Everything is included in order. Growth is shown by improvement, made from baseline to final unit evaluation. Followed IFP.

B – Everything is included. Growth is shown by improvement, made from baseline to final unit evaluation. Had some trouble following IFP.

C – One or two things are missing. It's tough to understand if there was any improvement. Had trouble following IFP.

D – The portfolio is tough to follow, and I can't tell if any improvement was made.

Self: What grade would you give your portfolio and why?

Peer: What grade would you give this portfolio and why?

In this case, the portfolio itself is being given a grade, which could be the student's grade for the unit. Or, the portfolio grade could be combined with the student's final unit evaluation and grade. With this portfolio grade, the teacher wouldn't have to look through each portfolio—the students already did that. The teacher could just look at the checklist to determine if anything is missing and if growth was communicated.

Again, we can't stress enough to start out small in the evaluation process. Some teachers indicated that they have over 400 students, and there is no way they have time to look over 400 portfolios. That's why we suggest maybe starting with one class, finding a way that works, then adding more classes as you feel more comfortable with the process. In grading, you may want at first to use the portfolio as a means of communication, and as you get more comfortable with the process, you can slowly wean yourself away from traditional grading and develop a system that works best for you and your students. Grading shouldn't be an overwhelming process. What we are shooting for is the students' taking over significant control in this area.

Ultimately, it would be great to move away from the whole letter-grading system in physical education and move more toward a checklist indicating specific skills and behaviors the students are doing well in and ones that need improvement. This approach would individualize physical education and move the focus toward personal growth. Whatever the process, we need to make sure the emphasis is geared to what's best for the student and what we can do to ignite a spark to get them turned on to fitness.

Assessment should not only help measure one's growth, it should facilitate that growth as well. When teachers use strategies such as student portfolios, they nurture and enrich the mind, body, and spirit of the students and promote a genuine interest in lifelong fitness and good health.

Appendix: Team Challenge Cards

CHALLENGE CARD
The Whole World

Equipment

- Cage ball, 48-inch or larger (1)
- Tires (2)

Starting Position

The group stands around the cage ball while the ball sits on the first tire.

Our Challenge

The challenge is mastered when the students successfully move the cage ball from tire to tire for a total of four trips back and forth.

Rules and Sacrifices

- The cage ball cannot touch the floor.
- The cage ball cannot touch the arms or hands of any group member.
- The ball must be moved from tire to tire a total of four times, and each attempt must be a different method of transfer than the last.
- If a rule is broken, the ball must be returned to the last successful tire, and the team must start again.
- No last names or put-downs.

From *Character Education* by D. Glover and L. Anderson, 2003, Champaign, IL: Human Kinetics.

ORGANIZER CARD
The Whole World

- What is our starting position?
- Where do we place the cage ball?
- What body parts cannot touch the ball?
- How many trips do we have to make with the ball?
- What happens if the ball touches the floor?
- What happens if we touch the ball with our hands or arms?

CHALLENGE CARD
Bridge Over The Raging River

Equipment

- Automobile tires, 14-inch (4)
- Two-by-fours, 8-foot (2)
- Jump ropes, or common clothesline, 6-8 feet (2)

Starting Position

All group members begin at the starting line at one end of the river with their equipment.

Our Challenge

This challenge is mastered when all group members have successfully crossed the river without breaking the rules and have brought all equipment with them.

Rules and Sacrifices

- Group members may not touch the floor.
- A group member may not step on a two-by-four if it has one end in the river.
- If a rule is broken, the group must take all equipment back to the starting position and start over.
- No last names or put-downs.

From *Character Education* by D. Glover and L. Anderson, 2003, Champaign, IL: Human Kinetics.

ORGANIZER CARD
Bridge Over the Raging River

Questions

- What equipment do we use?
- Where is our finish point?
- What happens if a person touches the floor?
- What happens if a two-by-four is in the river and someone steps on it?

CHALLENGE CARD
Knights of the Around Table

Equipment

- Sturdy table, 3-by-5-foot (1)
- Roll of gym-marking tape, or athletic tape (1)
- Large folding mats, 6-by-8-foot or 5-by-10-foot (2)

Starting Position

All group members start from behind the starting line, located 3 feet from the side of the table.

Our Challenge

When all group members have gone from the starting line, over the table, under the table, and again over the table, without touching the floor and are standing behind the finish line, the challenge has been successful.

Rules and Sacrifices

- If a group member touches the floor between the starting line and finish line, that person plus a sacrificed person must start over. (A sacrificed person is one that has already successfully gotten to the finish line.)
- Once a group member leaves the table and is standing behind the finish line, he or she may not get back on the table.

From *Character Education* by D. Glover and L. Anderson, 2003, Champaign, IL: Human Kinetics.

- Group members standing behind the starting line or the finish line may assist the group member attempting to go around the table, but they may not touch the table. (If the challenge is too difficult for your group, allow two other people, besides the person going around, to touch the table.) However, as soon as a fourth person touches the table, it is a failed attempt. Instructors need to watch the table and enforce the rule. This rule constantly forces kids to communicate.
- Negative pressure and put-downs are not allowed.
- No one may call a teammate by his of her last name.
- Safety note: Either the teacher or a designated student should help stabilize the table.

ORGANIZER CARD
Knights of the Around Table

Questions

- What happens if anyone touches the floor between the starting and finish lines?
- What happens if more than three people touch the table?
- If you get off the top of the table and make it to the finish line, can you get back on top of the table?
- What happens when you use negative pressure, put-downs, or last names?

CHALLENGE CARD
Juggler's Carry

Equipment

- Large rubber balls (4) (22-inch or larger) (or light rubber roto-molded balls, beach balls, cage balls)
- Long rope, 20-30 feet (1)
- Chairs (2)

Starting Position

The team starts behind the starting line. There are two balls behind this line and two balls behind the midcourt line.

From *Character Education* by D. Glover and L. Anderson, 2003, Champaign, IL: Human Kinetics.

Our Challenge

This challenge is mastered when all four balls have been picked up one at a time and have crossed the starting/finish line.

Rules and Sacrifices

- No ball may touch the floor between the end-court starting/finish line and the half-court line.
- Team members may not touch the balls with their hands.
- A different person or different group of people must pick up a ball and add it each trip.
- When traveling across the gym, all team members must be connected, and all team members must be touching a ball.
- No last names or put-downs.
- If any of these rules are broken, the team must start over from the line where the last successful trip was completed.

ORGANIZER CARD
Juggler's Carry

Questions

- What happens if a ball touches the floor between the starting/finish line and the half-court line?
- Must the team members be connected while transporting the balls?
- What happens if any team member touches the ball with his or her hands?
- Can the same two people pick up two balls in a row?

CHALLENGE CARD
Dynamic Barrier

Equipment

- Long jump rope (1)
- Large ball, 22-34 inches (1)
- Deck tennis rings (3) or beanbags (3)
- Hula hoop (1)
- Gym scooter (1)

From *Character Education* by D. Glover and L. Anderson, 2003, Champaign, IL: Human Kinetics.

Starting Position

The group must all be on one side of a twirling rope. Two members of the team are the temporary twirlers.

Our Challenge

The team must pass through the twirling barrier (rope) from one side to the other without touching the rope. In addition, all equipment must pass through the barrier as well. The twirlers must also pass through the barrier, so the group must decide when to change twirlers.

Rules and Sacrifices

- All group members and all equipment must pass through the barrier without touching it. The remaining rules are very important.
- The large ball must be rolled through, accompanied by a group member. In other words, a team member and the ball must pass through together, but the ball must be rolled.
- The deck tennis rings (or beanbags) must be tossed through the barrier and caught by a team member on the opposite side. If a ring is dropped, the team must start the challenge over from the beginning.
- The scooter must carry a team member through. The team must decide who will sit on the scooter and who will push through. *Caution:* Teammates may assist and push the scooter and their teammate through, but they must be aware of their proximity to the walls. As soon as the scooter gets through, the student should stop it to avoid coasting into other students or equipment.
- Two teammates must pass through at the same time while holding the hula hoop.
- All remaining students on the team must pass through the barrier together. They do not have to be connected, but they do have to pass through at the same time.
- If any teammate or any equipment touches the barrier, then that person or that piece of equipment—and all team members who have already successfully passed through the barrier—must go back.
- No last names or put-downs.

From *Character Education* by D. Glover and L. Anderson, 2003, Champaign, IL: Human Kinetics.

ORGANIZER CARD
Dynamic Barrier

Questions

- Where do we start our challenge? Where do we finish?
- How must the large ball pass through the barrier? How do the rings pass through? How must the hoop go through? How must the scooter pass through?
- Must the twirlers also pass through the barrier?
- What happens if any person or piece of equipment touches the barrier?

CHALLENGE CARD
Fling It

Equipment

- Large rubber ball, at least 22 inches (1) (the larger the ball, the more challenging this activity is)
- Ropes (used to transport the ball) (8)
- Base, or marker (to signify the fling-it spot) (1)

Starting Position

The team starts behind the starting line with the ball and ropes.

Our Challenge

Using only ropes, all group members must collectively transfer the ball from the starting point, around the midpoint, back to the starting point. When the ball reaches the fling-it point (base), about 15 feet from the ending point, they must fling it the rest of the way. The ball must be caught behind the line, by two teammates.

Rules and Sacrifices

- The ball must never touch the floor between the starting line and midpoint line.

From *Character Education* by D. Glover and L. Anderson, 2003, Champaign, IL: Human Kinetics.

- Teammates must not touch the ball with their hands or bodies after crossing the starting line and beginning the transport.
- Once the ball reaches the base on the return trip, it must be flung by using the ropes as flingers. The ball must be caught by two team members behind the starting line. The catchers, as designated by their team, may use their hands to catch the ball, but they must stay behind the starting line.
- The ball must be caught in the air by the catchers.
- No last names or put-downs.
- If any rule is broken, the team must return to the starting line and begin the challenge again.

ORGANIZER CARD
Fling It

Questions

- What equipment do we use?
- Can we touch the ball with our hands or bodies after crossing the starting line?
- When do we fling the ball?
- What happens if the catchers do not catch the ball behind the finish line?

CHALLENGE CARD
Frankenstein

Equipment

- Skeleton puzzle (1)
- Deck tennis ring (1)
- Storage crate (1)
- Indoor bases (5)

Starting Position

The team starts with one team member on each base with the other team members in the lab.

From *Character Education* by D. Glover and L. Anderson, 2003, Champaign, IL: Human Kinetics.

Our Challenge

The students are attempting to put together the skeleton puzzle in the fastest time possible. The team has to earn the right to put Frankenstein together by successfully tossing and catching a deck tennis ring. Each time the ring has been successfully passed, the team gets to add three more bones to Frankenstein. Seven trips of tossing the ring are required to build Frankenstein.

Rules and Sacrifices

- The deck tennis ring must be successfully tossed from base 1 to base 2. The person on base 2 must catch the ring and successfully turn and toss to the person on base 3. This process continues until the ring has traveled all the way to base 5 and back to base 1. If the ring is dropped, it must be sent back to the base that last tossed the ring.

- Once the ring gets back to base 1, the medic must run to the storage crate at the opposite end of the gym and bring back three bones. The medic cannot leave the Frankenstein-building area until the ring gets back to base 1.

- When the medic returns, he or she must give the bones to the doctors, who must start assembling the puzzle. When the doctors get the bones, all players need to rotate positions. The medic goes to base 1; base 1 goes to base 2; and so on. Base 5 becomes a new doctor, and one of the doctors becomes the new medic. Players cannot rotate positions until the medic returns to the Frankenstein-building area with three bones, the doctors place the bones in the correct position, and yell done.

- The ring needs to make seven successful round-trips to get all puzzle pieces to the building area. After the last medic has delivered the last three puzzle pieces, the team can hustle to the lab and confer as to any changes they need to make to Frankenstein to make him correct. When they think Frankenstein has been put together correctly, the last medic yells, "Lightning!" This is the signal to stop the clock. The teacher then checks the puzzle for accuracy. If it is correct, the time stands. If it is incorrect, the clock starts again as the team rearranges the bones. This process continues until Frankenstein is correct.

ORGANIZER CARD
Frankenstein

Questions

- What happens if we drop the ring during an attempted pass?
- What happens when the ring is successfully passed for one round?
- What happens when the doctor gets the bones from the medic?
- How many round-trips does the ring have to make to get all the bones into the lab?

CHALLENGE CARD
The Maze

Equipment

- Poly spots, 12-inch (16)
- Maze key cards

Starting Position

The team should line up behind the designated starting base. The leader should have the key and be far enough away from the rest of the team so that they are unable to view the key.

Our Challenge

The maze is mastered when all group members have successfully traveled from the starting point, through the maze, and out the designated ending point.

Rules and Sacrifices

- Team members may only continue if they take a correct step.
- The entire group must start over on a miss, even after one or more members have successfully completed the maze.
- Group members may not step on a base when it is not their turn.
- Each base may be used only once.
- Group members may not use last names or put-downs.

From *Character Education* by D. Glover and L. Anderson, 2003, Champaign, IL: Human Kinetics.

ORGANIZER CARD
The Maze

Questions

- What happens if someone takes an incorrect step?
- Can we step on any base twice?
- What happens if we get a yes-response from the leader?

CHALLENGE CARD
Toxic Splash

Equipment

- Small panel mats (3)
- Low balance beam (1)
- Small tire (1)
- Long poles, 5 to 7 feet (2)
- Plastic ice cream buckets (6)
- Items to fill the bucket (packing peanuts, golf balls, tennis balls, beanbags)
- Mats (to place around the beam for safety)

Our Challenge

All the team members and all the toxic materials must make it across the river and finish in the designated finishing area.

Rules and Sacrifices

- If a bucket touches any part of a team member's body, that team member plus a successful team member must return to the raft with their buckets of toxic materials.
- If any team member or any pole touches the river, the team member who made the error, plus one successful team member, must return to the raft with their buckets.
- If any toxic material spills out of the bucket into the river or on the land, the guilty team member who commits the error, plus an innocent bystander (another teammate), must be sacrificed.
- Only one person can be holding a pole at any time.

From *Character Education* by D. Glover and L. Anderson, 2003, Champaign, IL: Human Kinetics.

- The pole on the log and rock may not leave those places. They should remain on the log and rock after all toxic materials have been moved.
- Students should not use last names or put-downs.
- Any violation of any rule results in a one-plus-one sacrifice (the team-mate who erred plus one other).

ORGANIZER CARD
Toxic Splash

Questions

- Can the buckets of toxic waste touch any part of our bodies?
- What happens if a pole or any team member touches the water?
- What happens if any toxic material spills?
- How many teammates can be holding the pole at one time?
- Where will the poles be when our challenge is complete?

CHALLENGE CARD
Magic Bases

Equipment

Poly spots, 12-inch (one for each member of the team making the journey, plus one extra)

Our Challenge

The team must hold hands and travel through a figure-eight pattern of 12-inch poly spots. The team cannot speak, nor can they touch the floor. During this journey, the group has to communicate to figure out the best way to complete the journey, but they have to do so in some manner other than talking.

Rules and Sacrifices

- The team must travel the figure-eight route while holding hands. If they disconnect hands at any time, the whole group must start over.
- No more than two feet on a poly spot at one time.
- Team members may not touch the floor.
- No last names or put-downs.
- If any rule is broken, the group must start over.

From *Character Education* by D. Glover and L. Anderson, 2003, Champaign, IL: Human Kinetics.

ORGANIZER CARD
Magic Bases

Questions

- What happens if the team becomes disconnected?
- How many feet can be on a poly spot at one time?
- What happens if any team member touches the floor?

CHALLENGE CARD
Geo Sphere

Equipment

- Geo sphere (1)
- Multipurpose bucket (1)

Our Challenge

The team must set up the geo sphere so that it is balanced and upright in the bucket. The team must then plan the travel routes through the geo sphere without causing it to collapse.

Rules and Sacrifices

- The team members must travel through the geo sphere one at a time. Once one team member has used a pathway or specific entrance-to-exit route, that unique sequence of travel cannot be used by another team member. The same openings can be used but not in the same sequence.
- If a team member bumps the geo sphere, causing it to collapse, the entire team must start over from the beginning.
- Teammates may communicate and physically assist other teammates as they attempt to pass through.
- No one may stabilize the geo sphere to prevent its tipping over.
- No one may jump through the geo sphere.
- No last names or put-downs.

From *Character Education* by D. Glover and L. Anderson, 2003, Champaign, IL: Human Kinetics.

ORGANIZER CARD
Geo Sphere

Questions

- What happens if the geo sphere collapses?
- Can we hold the geo sphere with our hands?
- Can we use the same route through the geo sphere more than once?

CHALLENGE CARD
Rainbow Swamp Trail

Equipment

- Poly spots, 12-inch (12)
- Rainbow beanbags (6)

Our Challenge

Each member of the team must get to the other side of the swamp, but along the way, they each must retrieve a beanbag and take it with them to the shore. When all of the team members and all of the beanbags successfully make it to the opposite shore, the team has mastered the challenge.

Rules and Sacrifices

- The team must hold hands and stay connected throughout their trip through the swamp.
- No one may touch the floor during the trip through the swamp. If any rule is broken, the group must start over.
- Each team member must collect one beanbag on their journey and take it across the swamp.
- No last names or put-downs should be used during the challenge.

ORGANIZER CARD
Rainbow Swamp Trail

Questions

- What happens if any team member touches the floor?
- What happens if the team does not stay connected?

From *Character Education* by D. Glover and L. Anderson, 2003, Champaign, IL: Human Kinetics.

CHALLENGE CARD
Integrity Tower

Equipment

- Foam bricks (6), marked *Character, Respect, Sportspersonship, Judgment, Pride,* and *Integrity*

Our Challenge

The students must transport the foam blocks with a partner and build a tower at the designated site, 20 feet away.

Rules and Sacrifices

- Each block must be transported by two teammates. Each set of partners may only transport one block at a time.
- The blocks may never be touched by anyone's hands nor can the blocks ever touch the ground, except for the *Character* block, which must be the first block transported. All other blocks will be built upon the *Character* block.
- Each block must be transported using a different combination of body parts. No two partners can transport a block in the same method that other teammates did.
- For example, the first set of partners may use their elbows; the second set of partners may use their knees; and so on.
- Teammates may not help partners during the transport phase of the challenge, but they may help teammates stack the blocks on the tower as long as they don't use their hands. The teammates that transported the block must still be the principal stackers. They cannot relinquish control of the block, but teammates may assist them by steadying the tower or balancing a block while it is being placed.
- The *Integrity* block is the last block to be placed.
- No put-downs or last names are allowed.
- If any of these rules are broken, the group must take all blocks to the starting point.

From *Character Education* by D. Glover and L. Anderson, 2003, Champaign, IL: Human Kinetics.

ORGANIZER CARD
Integrity Tower

Questions

- How many people at a time are used to transport one brick?
- What happens if any brick falls to the ground?
- Can the *Character* brick touch the ground? Why?
- Can any bricks be transported the same way as others were?
- What happens if teammates touch a brick with their hands?
- Can teammates help stack the bricks when they arrive at the tower?

CHALLENGE CARD
Twist-and-Turn Marble Challenge

Equipment

- Twist-and-turn marble race track (1)
- Marbles (3)

Starting Position

Students should be connected to the tube at the waist and both wrists, then spaced out evenly for the entire length of the tube.

Our Challenge

When all three marbles have been passed through the entire length of the tube, the challenge is complete.

Rules and Sacrifices

- Team members may not touch the tube with their hands.
- The team must pass three marbles through the entire length of the tube without ever letting the marbles touch.
- No put-downs or last names.
- The first student in line may momentarily hold the tube to insert the marble.
- Teammates may physically assist one another.
- If any rule is broken, all three marbles must be returned to the first teammate, and the challenge starts over.

From *Character Education* by D. Glover and L. Anderson, 2003, Champaign, IL: Human Kinetics.

ORGANIZER CARD
Twist-and-Turn Marble Challenge

Questions

- What happens if teammates touch the tube with their hands?
- What happens if the marbles touch while inside the tube?
- Can teammates touch one another?

CHALLENGE CARD
Coconut Collection

Equipment

- River rafts (3)
- Gym scooters, 16-inch (6)
- Scooter paddles (6)
- Hula hoops (6)
- Balloons, 9-inch (24)

Starting Position

The team must start on the island with their river rafts and paddles.

Our Challenge

The team must paddle the rafts across the river, stopping at each of the islands to pick up coconuts. They must then deliver the coconuts to the opposite shore.

Rules and Sacrifices

- If a team member touches the floor, all river rafts must return to the starting line.
- If a balloon touches the floor, all river rafts must return to the starting line and all coconuts must be returned to the islands.
- All equipment must make it to shore (coconuts, paddles, and rafts).
- No put-downs or last names.

From *Character Education* by D. Glover and L. Anderson, 2003, Champaign, IL: Human Kinetics.

ORGANIZER CARD
Coconut Collection

Questions

- Can team members or coconuts touch the floor? What happens if they do?
- Do teams have to get all the equipment to the shore?

CHALLENGE CARD
The Great Pearl Caper

Equipment

- Pearl track transports (2)
- Large ball, 22-inch or larger (1)
- Tires, 15-inch (2)

Starting Position

All team members, along with the pearl track transports, start at the first tire, which is holding the giant pearl.

Our Challenge

The team must work together to transport the pearl across the gym with the pearl track transports. Then they must figure out how to place it in its pearl stand (the tire).

Rules and Sacrifices

- The pearl cannot be touched with any part of any team member's body.
- The pearl can only be transported by the pearl track transports.
- Once a team has the pearl in their track transport, that team cannot move toward the pearl stand. They can move anywhere when they are not in possession of the pearl.
- The pearl may never touch the ground.
- No put-downs or last names are allowed.
- If any rule is broken, the team must return to the starting line, replace the pearl on the tire, and attempt the challenge again.

From *Character Education* by D. Glover and L. Anderson, 2003, Champaign, IL: Human Kinetics.

ORGANIZER CARD
The Great Pearl Caper

Questions

- What happens if team members touch the pearl with their hands?
- What happens if the pearl touches the ground?
- Can you move toward the second tire if the pearl is in your track transport?

CHALLENGE CARD
Team Stomp It

Equipment

- Five-hole stomp-it board (1)
- Stomp-it balls (5)
- Table-tennis paddle (1)
- Poly spots (5)

Starting Position

The students gather around the team stomp-it board. The five balls should be on the board.

Our Challenge

Place five balls on a team stomp-it board. On signal, one teammate launches the balls into the air. All balls must be successfully caught, with each ball being caught by a different teammate. If the team accomplishes this, they may move to the second stage of the challenge. During the second stage, the stomper stomps one ball, then bats it into the air. This process of stomping and batting is repeated four times. Two of the four balls that were batted must be caught by teammates.

Rules and Sacrifices

- Each team member, including the stomper, must catch one ball. If any ball is dropped, the team must replace the balls and try again. If there are six team members, then the stomper is not required to catch a ball.

From *Character Education* by D. Glover and L. Anderson, 2003, Champaign, IL: Human Kinetics.

- Team members may not leave their poly spots until the stomper hits the stomp-it board.
- Everyone must rotate positions after each failed attempt.
- When all five balls are caught, the team selects a stomper/batter. The rest of the team must move their poly spots approximately 20 feet away from the side if the stomp-it board.
- Only one ball at a time can be used for batting. After it is struck, the catchers must make an attempt to catch the ball. Four balls are stomped and batted, two of which must be successfully caught for the challenge to be complete. If the team fails to catch two balls, they must start the challenge again from the beginning.

ORGANIZER CARD
Team Stomp It

Questions

- What happens if a ball is dropped after a stomp-and-catch attempt?
- How many balls must be stomped and batted?
- How many balls do we have to catch?
- What do we have to do if we don't succeed?

CHALLENGE CARD
Character Cup Stack

Equipment

- Buckets for stacking (12) (The teacher needs to write character-education words on one side of each bucket. These buckets could be the five-gallon buckets that you can get from your school's food service.)
- The Spanish translation of each character-education word should be written on the other side of the bucket. Here is a sample list of words:

From *Character Education* by D. Glover and L. Anderson, 2003, Champaign, IL: Human Kinetics.

English	Spanish
Respect	Respeto
Honesty	Honestidad
Tolerance	Tolerancía
Courage	Corage
Enthusiasm	Entusiasmo
Pride	Orgullo
Loyalty	Lealtad
Courtesy	Cortecía
To be an example	Ser un ejemplo
Character	Caracter
Caring	Protección
Integrity	Integridad

- The teacher should also write a number (1 through 12) on each bucket.
- Stacking keys (3)

Starting Position

The buckets and builders should be together in one area (the construction site), and the construction managers should be in the construction office with the construction key. The construction office should be located between the starting area and the construction site.

Our Challenge

When the six builders are ready, the construction managers instruct the builders in building a bucket tower according to the key. When the bucket tower has been built correctly and is approved by the teacher, the challenge is mastered.

Rules and Sacrifices

- Construction managers may not touch construction builders or buckets.
- Construction managers must stay in the construction office.
- Construction builders may only move one bucket at a time to the construction site.
- Construction manager may not use the terms *line, on top of, front, behind,* or *next to.*

From *Character Education* by D. Glover and L. Anderson, 2003, Champaign, IL: Human Kinetics.

- No one should use put-downs or call other teammates by last names.
- If any of these rules are broken, the buckets must be returned to the starting area.

ORGANIZER CARD
Character Cup Stack

Questions

- Can the construction managers touch the builders or buckets?
- How many buckets can be moved and stacked at a time?
- What happens if these rules are broken?

CHALLENGE CARD
Raiders of the Lost Jewel

Equipment

- Large cone, 12-24 inches (1)
- Dowels, wood or metal, or track batons, 18-24 inches (2)
- Cloth ropes (4) (the length of which should be slightly shorter than the center circle diameter)
- Center circle on a basketball court, or make a large circle out of rope (about 10 feet in diameter)

Starting Position

Place the cone in the center of the circle with the ball balanced on top. The team members and every other piece of equipment should be on the outside of the circle.

Our Challenge

The team must figure out how to get the lost jewel out of the jungle and back to its rightful place in the museum of lost jewels. They must remove the jewel from its resting place and get it to the museum, which is outside the center circle on a basketball court. The team must perform this rescue three times, and the team must rescue the jewel a different way each time.

From *Character Education* by D. Glover and L. Anderson, 2003, Champaign, IL: Human Kinetics.

Rules and Sacrifices

- No group member may step inside the circle at any point during the challenge.
- The ball may not touch the ground inside or outside the circle.
- The ball must be successfully removed from the circle three times, each time a different way.
- No one can use last names or put-downs.
- If any rule is broken, the ball must return to the starting point, and that effort must be repeated.

ORGANIZER CARD
Raiders of the Lost Jewel

Questions

- What happens if any group member steps inside the circle?
- Can the ball ever touch the ground?
- How many times do team members have to move the ball outside the circle?
- What happens if a teammate breaks a rule?

CHALLENGE CARD
Factor In

Equipment

- Round bases, with numbers written or taped on top (12)

Starting Position

The team should be at the entrance to the maze, connected, and ready to enter.

Our Challenge

The team must remain connected and move through a maze of numbered bases. The team members must stand on various bases in the maze, but the bases they are using must have a total number that can be factored by three.

From *Character Education* by D. Glover and L. Anderson, 2003, Champaign, IL: Human Kinetics.

The task is mastered when all group members move from the entrance of the maze to the exit while remaining connected, and they must keep the sum total of the bases a factor of three.

Rules and Sacrifices

- Team members must stay connected during travel.
- Team members may only move one base at a time.
- Team members may move in either a straight or diagonal path.
- Teammates may not be two bases away from the immediate person they are connected to.
- Only one team member may enter the maze at a time. When teammates get to the last row of the maze, they must stay connected, but they may step out of the maze.
- After each team member enters or exits the maze, the total-sum number (of the bases team members are standing on) must be a factor of three. Otherwise, the team must start again.
- Only one person on a base at a time.
- No one should call others by their last names or use put-downs.
- If any rule is broken, the team must go back to the entrance and start again.

ORGANIZER CARD

Factor In

Questions

- Do teammates have to stay connected during travel?
- How many bases can one person move at a time?
- The sum total of all the bases that the teammates are standing on must be a factor of what number?
- Can teams have more than one person on a base at one time?
- What happens if a team member breaks a rule?

From *Character Education* by D. Glover and L. Anderson, 2003, Champaign, IL: Human Kinetics.

References

Billings, L. 2002. *White House finally on the right exercise track*. St. Paul Pioneer Press, 25 June.

Bloom, B.S. (Ed.) 1956. *Taxonomy of educational objectives: The classification of educational goals*. New York: Longmans, Green.

Caine, G. and R. Caine. 1994. *Making connections: Teaching and the human brain*. New York: Addison Wesley.

Covey, S. 1989. *The seven habits of highly effective people*. New York: Simon & Schuster.

Covey, S. 2000. *The seven habits of highly effective people, miniature edition*. Philadelphia: Running Press.

Dahl, K. 1998. Reflection and passion in teaching. Unpublished.

Ebbock, V., and S. Gibbons. 1998. Team-building study. University of Oregon and University of Victoria.

Glasser, W. 1998. *Choice theory: A new psychological freedom*. New York: Harper-Perennial.

Glover, D., and D. Midura. 1992. *Team building through physical challenges*. Champaign, IL: Human Kinetics.

Goldman, D. 1997. *Emotional intelligence*. New York: Bantam Books.

Jensen, E. 2000. *Brain-based learning*. San Diego: The Brain Store.

Katz, L. 1993. All about me. *American Educator* 17(2): 18-23.

Kilpatrick, M., E. Herbert, and D.Jacobsen. 2002. Physical activity motivation: A practitioner's guide to self-determination theory. *JOPERD* 73(4): 37-41.

Kohn, A. 1992. *No contest: The case against competition*. Boston: Houghton Mifflin.

Kohn, A. 1993. *Punishment by rewards*. Boston: Houghton Mifflin.

Kriete, R. 1999. *The morning meeting book*. Greenfield, MA: The Northeast Foundation for Children.

Kulinna, P.H., W. Zhu, M. Behnke, R.O. Johnson, D. McMullen, M.E. Turner, and G. Wolff. 1999. Six steps in developing and using fitness portfolios. *Teaching Elementary Physical Education* 10(5): 15-17.

Lickona, T. 1991. *Educating for character: How our schools can teach respect and responsibility.* New York: Bantam.

Martens, R. 1977. *Joy and sadness in children's sports.* Champaign, IL: Human Kinetics.

Melograno, V. 1998. *Professional and student portfolios for physical education.* Champaign, IL: Human Kinetics.

Michener, J.A. 1976. *Sports in America.* New York: Ballantine Books.

Midura, D., and D. Glover. 1995. *More team building challenges.* Champaign, IL: Human Kinetics.

Midura, D. and D. Glover. 1999. *The competition-cooperation link.* Champaign, IL: Human Kinetics.

Mohnsen, B. 1998. Assessing and grading middle school students. *Teaching Elementary Physical Education* 9(6): 13-15.

Odyssey of the Mind newsletter. Fall 1995: 5.

Parson, Monica. 2001. Enthusiasm and feedback: A winning combination. *PE Central.* [Online]. www.pecentral.org/climate/monicaparsonarticle.html

Ralbovsky, M. 1974. *Lords of the locker room: The American way of coaching and its effect on youth.* New York: Peter H. Wyden.

Rogers, S., J. Ludington, and S. Graham. 1998. *Motivation and learning.* Evergreen, CO: Peak Learning Systems.

Rogers, S. and L. Renard. 1999. Relationship-driven teaching. *Educational Leadership* 57(1): 34-37.

Schaps, E., C. Lewis, and M.Watson. 1996. Building community in school. *Principal* 76: 29-31.

Schneider, E. 1996. Giving students a voice in the classroom. *Educational Leadership* 54(1): 22-25.

Tileston, D.W. 2000. *10 best teaching practices: How brain research, learning styles, and standards define teaching competencies.* Thousand Oaks, CA: Corwin Press.

About the Authors

Don Glover has taught physical education, including adapted physical education, since 1967 at the preschool, elementary, secondary, and postsecondary levels. He currently teaches elementary physical education methods at the University of Wisconsin at River Falls.

In 1981 Glover was recognized as Minnesota's Teacher of the Year and was named the Minnesota Adapted Physical Education Teacher of the Year in 1989. He has written three books, published numerous magazine and journal articles on physical education and sport, and has been a clinician at more than 100 workshops and clinics.

Glover earned his master's degree in physical education from Winona State University in 1970. A former president of MAHPERD, he is also a member of AAHPERD, NASPE, COPEC, and the Minnesota Education Association.

Leigh Anderson currently facilitates the master's of education program at Saint Mary's University using many of the concepts presented in this book. She earned a master's degree in curriculum and instruction from Hamline University in St. Paul, Minnesota, and she is a former classroom teacher in the West St. Paul school district.